GEORGE FABYAN

The Tycoon Who Broke Ciphers, Ended Wars, Manipulated Sound, Built a Levitation Machine, and Organized the Modern Research Center

BY RICHARD MUNSON

Porter Books

Copyright © 2013 Richard Munson
All rights reserved.

ISBN: 1490345620
ISBN-13: 9781490345628

Library of Congress Control Number: 2013911932
CreateSpace Independent Publishing Platform
North Charleston, South Carolina

TABLE OF CONTENTS

The Colonel	1
Wanderings	15
Chicago	23
Riverbank	47
Acoustics	65
Ciphers, Shakespeare, and Levitation	93
Spies and Warfare	111
Withdrawal	141
Legacy	161
Acknowledgements	165
About the Author	167
Endnotes	169

Chapter 1
THE COLONEL

The rich are different, but George Fabyan was unique among millionaires.

This Gilded Age tycoon sponsored and inspired a "community of thinkers" who advanced science in such diverse fields as acoustics, cryptography, genetics, and physiology. Yet the whimsical Fabyan also tried to construct a levitation machine that would defy gravity, and he spent millions trying to prove Sir Francis Bacon wrote Shakespeare's plays.

Considering himself an "ideas man," Fabyan changed how we wage wars and keep secrets, how we transmit sound and design buildings, and how we stimulate scientific advances. He created perhaps the first independent research center, laid the foundation for the top-secret National Security Agency, and even helped end World War I by breaking German codes, capturing foreign terrorists, and developing more effective trench mortars.

Rather than seek profits or teach students, Fabyan's Riverbank Laboratories examined concepts for their own sake or, perhaps more accurately, for how they tickled his fancy. With a highly successful cloth and dry-goods business and the means to explore his many interests, Fabyan

GEORGE FABYAN

said, "We tackle problems which the universities haven't the money or the time to tackle." In addition to serious endeavors on codes and sounds, he developed "cob-less corn" for the toothless and tried to help women of his generation overcome what he called "debutante slouch."

Preferring the honorary title of "colonel" he obtained from Illinois's governor for mostly ceremonial duties, Fabyan displayed an almost childlike curiosity, and he explored questions – whether about acoustics, ciphers, bees, or bells – with great joy and enthusiasm. He viewed himself as "mankind's servant – for the fun of it,"[1] balancing social commitment with humor.

Commenting on Riverbank's cerebral carnival, the colonel stated, "The world is full of mysteries and the greatest adventure is life itself." No doubt the exuberant Fabyan loved living. He savored his Phillip Morris's as well as his cases of Scotch and wine, and he relished motion pictures, particularly Westerns, as well as women.

The colonel, however, dismissed a life of leisure and turned up his nose at lazy millionaires. "Some rich men go in for art collections, gay times on the Riviera, or extravagant living. But they all get satiated," he said. "That's why I stick to scientific experiments, spending money to discover valuable things that universities can't afford. You never get sick of too much knowledge."

Fabyan had no interest in being satiated or bored, so he pursued his interests vigorously. Drawn to zoology, he stocked his Illinois estate with exotic animals, including two bears (named Tom and Jerry), a gorilla (named Hamlet), alligators, and red-suited monkeys, and he built a lavish kennel for show-champion dogs as well as Louie, a wolf he said provided "security." Fabyan also spent what today would be almost two million dollars to buy and move a Dutch windmill because he liked its look and its ability to grind the various grains devised in his genetics laboratory, where he tested a range of theories, including whether seeds planted during a full moon would produce greater yields.

Despite such odd habits, Fabyan acquired an impressive list of professional awards. Probably no other American received the French Medal of

Honor, Japan's Order of the Rising Sun, as well as commendations from the U.S. National Security Agency. Few millionaires can claim to have negotiated an international treaty to end a war. No other businessman housed the American military's center for code breaking, and virtually no science patron advanced research in such disparate fields.

At six feet, four inches, Fabyan presented an imposing figure that conveyed his own outsized ambitions. His iron-gray hair, arched right eyebrow, and dark, full mustache added to his air of superiority. He also used clothing to assume various buccaneer roles, often sporting frayed riding clothes and knee-high boots, for instance, in order to appear rugged and adventurous, some said like Ernest Hemingway. When not feeling like a horseman, he would become a yachtsman – complete with blue blazer, white shoes, and turtleneck sweater – although no one at his Riverbank estate remembered him riding or sailing.

Loud, with a hearty laugh, the colonel pronounced, in response to a question about what he raised on his 350-acre Riverbank estate in a western-Chicago suburb, "I raise hell." Put more politely, Fabyan stimulated inquisitiveness. He identified and motivated smart people, asked them probing questions and encouraged them to challenge established theories. He directed this avant-garde faculty to "wrestle from Nature her secrets," and he drew connections among his team's diverse research. According to one scholar, the colonel "was quick to learn the relevant terminology and to acquire knowledge of the subject matter."[2] Another said the mogul "had the natural gifts of energy and dynamism."[3]

Fabyan, although he never graduated from high school, thought of himself as a scientist, a man willing to test ideas for the good of humanity. Colleagues described him as "intelligent," "ahead of his time," and possessing a "high degree of scientific curiosity," yet he also was known as "colorful," "non-conformist," and "paternalistic." One Riverbank resident, commenting on the colonel's mixed personality, said his "seemingly gruff exterior hid a passionate, inquisitive desire to explore the countless mysteries of life."[4]

GEORGE FABYAN

This patron of science, according to one colleague, ruled "one of the strangest institutions in the world." Compared to many of his millionaire colleagues who were riding horses on their massive estates or lounging at expensive resorts, Fabyan's "art was in positive, tangible value, even in fun. He converted hobbies into social service."[5]

Scientific American literally gushed about Riverbank's varied research efforts, claiming Fabyan's team "will unfold to us wonders within the next few years. We shall learn more about the human body than ever before; we shall wrest certain secrets from nature which have never been suspected; a new epoch will most likely open up."[6] *Fortune Magazine* subsequently ranked Fabyan one of history's ten most interesting millionaires.

Several turn-of-the-century barons believed their riches should be tempered by obligation. Andrew Carnegie, for instance, created libraries, John D. Rockefeller established universities, and J.P. Morgan launched museums. Yet these tycoons focused primarily on their steel, oil, and banking empires, and only later in life did they give away some of their riches. In contrast, Fabyan's chief passion throughout his life was the Riverbank think tank. Making money from selling cloth and clothes was only a means to explore questions that interested him.

The colonel certainly mingled freely with Chicago's business elite, including Joy Morton (salt), Marshall Field (merchandise), William Wrigley (gum), Philip Armour (meat), George Pullman (railcars), Francis Peabody (coal), Samuel Insull (electricity), and Cyrus McCormick (harvesters). They elected him to the Chicago Stock Exchange, the Union League, and the Chicago and South Shore Country Clubs. Yet the so-called cotton king stood apart, largely because his real love was science rather than business or money. Although a consummate salesman who expanded a profitable dry-goods empire, he decided by the end of the 19th century he had earned "enough."

Fabyan created the first independent science research center focused on disparate disciplines. Private and public universities in the early 20th century certainly assembled diverse scholars to examine new ideas, but their underlying goal tended to be teaching. The Scripps Institute in San Diego conducted first-rate research, but it focused just on oceanography. Thomas Edison's Menlo Park laboratory developed numerous technologies, such as the light bulb and phonograph, but the wizard's purpose was profit. Riverbank Laboratories, in contrast, explored wide-ranging ideas largely because they fascinated Fabyan and might prove useful to others.

Like most powerful men, the colonel displayed a mix of characteristics, but his wealth tended to exaggerate both his attributes and his eccentricities. One of Fabyan's most obvious traits was a wry sense of humor. For instance, his one writing project, a book entitled *What I Know About the Future of Cotton and Domestic Goods*, contained 100 blank pages. The author's note in that publication jokingly explained: "Yielding to the many requests of friends the author has consented to inflict on the public this Second Edition."[7]

Peeved he had to obtain an act of Congress to build a bridge linking his properties on both banks of the Fox River, which the Army Corps of Engineers declared was navigable even though it ran less than four feet deep in most spots, Fabyan constructed a copper-domed lighthouse on his island in order to guide the non-existent navigators. Demonstrating his desire for sly fun, the colonel arranged for the lamp to blink out a beam sequence of two, then three, then two, then three – Fabyan's way of saying "keep out" with the old expression "Twenty three skidoo." The colonel also christened his island the "Isle of View;" dedicated to his wife Nelle, the name spoken rapidly became his pronouncement of affection.

Another example of Fabyan's dry wit was the sign he mounted beside Riverbank's office entrance asking visitors to "Ring Bell for Service." To their surprise, pulling the strap launched a heavy clapper that swung wildly and loudly. Embarrassed guests tended to stand shell shocked for the 10-15 seconds it took for the din to subside, and only then would the smiling colonel appear.

Despite such childish pranks, Fabyan was distinguished enough President Theodore Roosevelt asked him in 1905 to serve on the team – as

GEORGE FABYAN

liaison to Japanese officials – negotiating the end to the Russo-Japanese War, a process that earned the president the Nobel Peace Prize. This Treaty of Portsmouth – which recognized Japan's influence in the Chinese province of Manchuria and required Russia to give up half of the Sakhalin Island – allowed Roosevelt to end the conflict but also to limit Tokyo's political and economic clout in Asia.

Another attribute in Fabyan's personality arsenal was generosity. During recessions and depressions, despite his own substantial losses, the colonel gave to a local grocer a list of supplies for needy families. The merchant was to deliver those provisions weekly, yet he could never reveal the benefactor's name without losing Fabyan's business. Also on the sly, the colonel helped several local merchants reopen their businesses, and he paid a group of out-of-work men to dig ditches and perform other chores at Riverbank. Each new baby on the estate, moreover, received a ten-dollar gold coin from the colonel, and children often followed Fabyan around the grounds because "he was always good for a shiny dime."[8]

Yet the domineering colonel also expected to get his way. He would bark out orders and rant his displeasures, often from one of Riverbank's two "hell chairs" — an Egyptian-style concrete armchair that sat atop the estate's west hill, near the villa, and a wicker seat that swung from chains on the house's veranda. From these thrones, the colonel offered stern directives and animated complaints about Riverbank's operations. According to a researcher, "The colonel sat and swung back and forth, chain smoking and poking an enormous fire which burned even on summer evenings. Evening after evening he sat there with anyone he could gather around, and if anyone in the conversation would displease him he would stand the offending person, guest, or employee up before the hell chair and literally give them hell. Thus the name."[9]

Fabyan could be brusque and awkward. One employee said he possessed an energetic laugh but "created situations that were often open to criticism."[10] Another stated, "He was the kind of man who did not take 'no' for an answer."[11] Sumiko Kobayashi, the gardener's young daughter, experienced first-hand Fabyan's gruff ways when she was playing in the pool's shallow end with other children of Riverbank employees. The colonel, on one of his inspecting strolls throughout the estate, noticed Sumiko was the only child not venturing into the deep water. Convinced he knew the best way to teach her to swim, he ordered Sumiko to jump off the diving board. The petrified girl begged, but the colonel barked out his order more loudly. She eventually jumped, promptly panicked, and began to sink. Others rushed in to save the young girl from drowning while the oblivious Fabyan continued on his rounds.

Several staff came to balk at the colonel's authoritarian ways and tyrannical oversight, while some complained he tried to take credit for their work. Yet most Riverbank employees found the colonel to be a generous benefactor. According to one, they enjoyed the genteel life of the "minor idle rich."[12] As an example, researchers every evening received by their bed a glass of ice water and a bowl of fruit.

Fabyan, not surprisingly, didn't see himself as overbearing. "I am not capable of bossing your work or you," he wrote to a new employee, "but I am capable of recognizing hard, earnest, sincere endeavor, whether it results in success or not." He consistently identified himself to reporters as simply part of a team. "We're all working together," he said. "No bosses, no time clocks, no cast iron regulations. I, too, am just a worker."[13] Suggesting equality among researchers, Fabyan declared, in his folksy way, "We're all thinkers out here. Yes-siree, every one of the 150 souls in the Riverbank community."[14] Despite such self-deprecating comments, Fabyan mastered some combination of dictator and motivator that won him the grudging loyalty of a diverse, talented, as well as testy and high-strung group of scientists.

The colonel also displayed a patriotic militarism, although he never served in the armed forces. Fabyan raised and lowered the Riverbank flag each day with bugles and pomp, he required his workmen at 11:00 am sharp to be in the north fields for a half hour of marching and drilling, and he paid for uniforms and an instructor to train the boys of Geneva High

GEORGE FABYAN

School in military discipline and tactics. The colonel also sponsored the Fox River Guards, hired military instructors, dug three miles of trenches, and taught the volunteers methods of modern trench fighting, while his researchers helped develop and test mortars and triton hand grenades, weapons that provided clear advantages to the allies in World War I. To ensure the first, second, and third line trenches were authentic, Fabyan hired Samuel Allison, a Canadian private who had seen two years of active service in France and was a hero of the battle of Ypres.

In July 1917, the patriotic colonel even staged at Riverbank a large recruiting program – complete with demonstrations on mortars, gas masks, and care of the wounded – that attracted almost 5,000 people.[15] After hearing an army captain's 30-minute speech, inspired young men headed to the recruitment tent, as described by the local newspaper, "like sinners hitting the trail at the apex of a Billy Sunday peroration, others sprang up in every portion of the packed outdoor gathering and pressed through as the thousands arose and screamed with ecstasy."[16]

Chance encounters with the colonel revealed something of a natural teacher. One young girl in 1930 was visiting a family friend near Fabyan's windmill when the colonel happened to walk by and invited them to see his animals. Remembering the colonel as "a very kind and gracious man," the girl said he brought out a snake and encouraged her to touch it. "He was so kind to explain about the snake," she later stated. "He even brought out an egg and showed how a snake will disengage his jaw to accommodate something as large as an egg. He was showing us a wonderful science experiment."[17]

Another young woman, whose father worked on the estate, recalled meeting the colonel when he was out inspecting his gardens and dressed in a white cable-knit sweater and white trousers. "Our dog jumped up on him and soiled his clothes," the embarrassed woman remembered. "My mother was absolutely horrified, but he never said a thing about it. He just continued on his way across the street to work at the laboratory."[18]

"Knowledge is Power"

Fabyan, at his core, displayed passionate curiosity. He sought to understand how sound traveled and was absorbed, how radiation could highlight and cure the human body, how genetically engineered grains could feed the hungry, and how secrets could be kept or deciphered.

The colonel's inquisitiveness ranged widely, from bells to bombs and howitzers to hearing aids. He was, according to one reporter, "the gentlemen's bad-boy" who was "at the forefront of progressive development."[19] In his own words, in a letter to William Friedman as the researcher began work at Riverbank: "If I should hear of something anywhere this side of Hell that I thought would do us any good, I might want you to go there and find out about it. In other words, I don't want to go backwards."[20]

Fabyan's explorations, if not exactly moving in reverse, sometimes wandered and sparked out-of-the-ordinary projects. To test his thought that "busy" bees might actually be lazy, he built a glass-walled hive in his house. As the colonel informed a visiting journalist, "Those bees are just going into the music room to deposit their honey. You see I didn't trust that particular bunch of bees," he continued, "so I had their hive placed inside the (villa) and had it glassed in so we could watch them and see that they didn't cheat. They go in through a hole in the wall. It's made honest bees out of them – this constant supervision."[21]

Yet even the odd endeavors often provided valuable and practical insights. To answer his wife's off-handed question about whether England or the United States made better bells, Fabyan ordered the construction of temperature-compensated tuning forks that could accurately measure sound quality. Because of their ability to also synchronize transmitters and receivers, those sophisticated tools made possible the Associated Press's first long-distance photographic facsimile, and they regulated the frequency of electricity generated at Hoover Dam and other power plants.

Fabyan sometimes wagered on his research, as he did with "one of my wealthy Jewish friends" on a genetics project to develop grain seeds that would flourish in deserts. The image-oriented colonel stated, "I want the father of wheat, and I want a wife for him, so that the child will grow in arid country." If successful in this effort to increase the world's food supply, Fabyan said his friend "will foot the bills and be damned glad to."[22]

Conventional thinking was to be avoided. "I have seen impracticable and improbable things accomplished," the colonel wrote, "providing the direction was practical and based on sound business principles." Fabyan, of course, remained confident he could supply the needed direction and principles.

That guidance inspired several of Riverbank's scientists to dominate their fields. Wallace and Paul Sabine, for instance, designed the world's premier reverberation chamber to study the acoustical properties of doors, drapes, and other architectural materials. They also developed highly precise tuning forks that advanced wireless communications, alternating current machinery, and geophysical measurements. For such leadership, Wallace Sabine's colleagues voted to name a standard acoustical measurement after him.

William and Elizebeth Friedman, meanwhile, literally wrote the books on codes and ciphers, and they built the early computers that crafted and broke them. They also trained the U.S. military's code specialists during World War I, and they laid the foundation for the highly secret National Security Agency.

The colonel maintained two mottos: the Francis Bacon declaration – "Knowledge is power" – and his own observation – "We play the game from day to day the best we can." Fabyan had the resources both to acquire knowledge and to play the game with flair. He inherited $3 million from his father – a princely sum in the early 20th century, worth almost $70 million today – as well as control of what he made into an even more prosperous textile company.

With that money, he hired a diverse set of experts. In addition to the Sabines and Friedmans, he contracted with a prominent veterinary surgeon to seek a cure for hoof-and-mouth disease, which had been destroying cattle throughout the nation's heartland. He employed J.A. Powell, the former editor of the University of Chicago Press, to write papers on typography, and he attracted leading geneticists to develop drought-resistant grains as well as "cob-less corn."

The colonel played his game with optimism, frequently putting setbacks in perspective. "Failure is going to come," he noted, "and a lot of them, and a lot of disappointment, loss after loss, but as long as it is done intelligently, and we know why, I have no kick coming."[23]

No doubt bright, Fabyan relied more on instinct than intellect. As he put it, "I do not go ahead unless I have had a hunch."[24] He seemed to be drawn to ideas – from the cracking of codes to the debunking of Shakespeare – more on the passion with which they were advanced than with their rationality.

The colonel also used his intuition to evaluate people. "One of the greatest qualifications for success in any walk of life," he wrote, "is the ability to judge human nature and men."[25] Fabyan prided himself on that ability, and he often proved to be a harsh judge. Of one interviewee, he wrote she "proved to be a lemon of the first water. ... She surely made a holy show of herself. She isn't even housebroke."[26]

Fabyan justified Riverbank's work with hyperbole and visions. When asked about his genetics work on roses and tulips, the colonel declared, "Look at the average human being, a plightly pitiful contraption of flesh and bones. If we the Riverbank community can improve the human race by experimenting first with flowers and plants ... say, won't that be a wonderful thing?"[27]

Expanding the Fabyan family's interest in pathology, he paid particular attention to "what's wrong with the human body." His quick history of human progression was: "Man started as a wiggling snake, became a tadpole, acquired shoulders somehow, grew into an anthropoid ape, and then decided to stand up, walk on his hind legs, and become a man." The physiological problem with this evolution, the colonel said, was "our stomachs were made to be carried horizontally, not vertically. Look at all the sickness that's come from defying nature!" Fabyan maintained his research would relieve that sickness and allow everyone to live to be 100 years old. "Just wait awhile," he boasted. "We're working it out."[28] Among the colonel's other benevolent efforts were radiation therapy to combat cancer, experimentation with X-rays, and the development of hearing aids. Several dying cancer patients, for example, left their hospitals for the promise of radium treatments at Riverbank.

Outside his laboratories, the colonel's diverse interests included collecting Asian (particularly Japanese) paintings and sculpture, some of which is displayed at the Art Institute of Chicago. He assembled a substantial compilation of ancient texts, more than a thousand volumes of which were donated to the Library of Congress. He designed and built several of his estate's innovative buildings, and he worked with Frank Lloyd Wright to reform his villa. The engineering lab, in fact, reveals one of the colonel's more unique hobbies – the purchase, sight unseen, of unclaimed freight from Chicago's railroad yards. One especially large acquisition included carloads of 15-foot I beams, which motivated Fabyan to devise the pyramided structure with rooms measuring 15-by-15 feet.

Attracting Attention

Fabyan referred to himself as a private and shy person, and he certainly advanced secrecy throughout society, yet he and Riverbank frequently attracted attention. The colonel regularly invited reporters to tour his estate and laboratories, and the flashy tycoon, wrote one journalist, "dressed the part of a millionaire country gentleman. He wore a frock coat, fancy vest, lavender stock around his neck, and bowler hat. … In his coat lapel he wore the rosette of the Legion of Honor of France."[29]

Tall, straight, and handsome, Fabyan appeared imposing. A local newspaper described him as "a blond giant of the north in the garb of today, with a tawny beard and flashing blue eyes and a physique which was most impressive."[30]

THE COLONEL

With movie-star looks, the colonel enjoyed entertaining a wide variety of celebrities, including Theodore Roosevelt, Albert Einstein, P.T. Barnum, Flo Ziegfield and his wife Billie Burke, Mary Pickford, and Admiral Richard Byrd. Roosevelt considered Fabyan a friend and the two spent many hours discussing Japan, genetics, and agriculture. Einstein went out of his way to visit the Riverbank Laboratories and to commend Fabyan's commitment to science. Barnum and Ziegfield appreciated the colonel's showmanship.

Most evenings, George and wife Nelle hosted dinner parties for some 20 people, including Chicago's elite, Riverbank researchers, and visiting luminaries. Since the Fabyans didn't enjoy travel, they brought the world to them, and many of the revelers stayed in one of Riverbank's guest houses since the colonel did not like visitors spending the night in his villa.

Warm evenings were spent before one of the outdoor fire pits, where Fabyan orchestrated questions to his researchers and guests who were expected to deliver stimulating conversation. A rainy night might find the colonel and his friends in his private box at the Arcada, the nearby movie theater, where he rarely missed a new release.

The colonel sometimes entered national controversies. When the media hounded Joy Morton's niece after her affair with the family's jockey, for instance, the colonel offered Riverbank as Helen Morton's sanctuary, and he hired guards to keep the press hoards at bay. One enterprising reporter for the *Chicago Journal* – Lowell Thomas, who became a well-known broadcaster and the traveler who made Lawrence of Arabia famous – devised a scheme whereby he would float down the Fox River, enter the estate, and convince Helen to recount her lovelorn tales. The newspaper printed the heiress-jockey story to the delight of the nation's scandal-hungry masses, but Thomas later admitted he couldn't get by Fabyan's defenses and said, "We had simply invented the whole thing."[31]

Fabyan had his own run-in with a photographer from the *Chicago Journal* outside the Geneva train station where the colonel was picking up Helen's father. According to the xenophobic local newspaper, "The Jap snapped his camera three times close to (Fabyan's) face, all the time in front of him. The third time (Fabyan) became enraged, took the lad by the coat collar, none too gently, grabbed the camera out of his hands, smashed it on the bricks three times and kicked it."[32]

The colonel was charged with assault and disorderly conduct and appeared in court with Joy Morton and Helen's father. "I did not hit him or hurt him at all," testified the colonel. The Salt King also took the stand to complain about how the media had been harassing his family and invading his privacy. The trial, according to the *Geneva Republican*, featured "a whole lot of cheap talk by Chicago attorneys" representing the big-city media, yet the local judge ordered Fabyan to pay a meager $3 for "assaulting the Jap photographer."[33]

George not only protected Helen, who affectionately referred to him as "Daddy Long Legs," he offered to host her wedding at Riverbank. Yet the prospect of a jockey for a son-in-law sparked "a fusillade of angry telegrams from her father and entreating letters from her mother." Still, the popular debutante proceeded with the ceremony, and her father eventually relented, even "smilingly (giving) the couple his blessing."[34] Not long after the ceremony, however, Helen's family challenged the marriage and claimed she was mentally deranged. A court eventually agreed, identified the colonel as Helen's guardian, and ordered the young bride to move into an asylum.

Such Fabyan's controversies, however, cannot detract from his accomplishments. The curious colonel changed his world, bringing science to acoustics and secrecy to war. He stimulated diverse research and achieved diplomatic success. While reflecting his era's fascination with science and quest for knowledge, Fabyan's was a unique journey.

Chapter 2
WANDERINGS

The colonel descended from New England Brahmins. His Puritan ancestors, in fact, emigrated from England in the 1640's, and seven generations of Fabyans prospered in communities within New Hampshire, Maine, and Massachusetts

Fabyan's parents, George Francis and Isabella, belonged to the region's best institutions, including Boston's Union Club, Marblehead's Eastern Yacht Club, and Brookline's Country Club. Noted for his "great keenness in financial and business matters, of strict integrity and high standing," the senior Fabyan also joined the Metropolitan Club of New York City and was one of the few northeastern members of Georgia's Jekyl Island Club.[35]

George Francis, despite a substantial inheritance from his physician father, began his work life as an errand boy and traveling salesman. He invested wisely and eventually bought a small company, renamed it Bliss Fabyan & Company, and turned it into the nation's largest dry good merchandiser that also operated cotton mills producing textiles. He also became perhaps Boston's largest real estate owner, and he served as a director or trustee with Merchants National Bank of Boston, Old Colony Trust Company, and Metropolitan Storage Warehouse Company.

GEORGE FABYAN

When not making money selling fabric, cloth, and real estate, George Francis rode horses, captained his specially designed yacht, managed a Brookline estate, and raised rare flowers that won numerous awards from the Massachusetts Horticultural Society. An aggressive philanthropist, he contributed $250,000 (now equivalent to $6.4 million) to the Harvard Medical School in order to endow a chair, named after his own father, in comparative pathology.

Fabyan's business partner, Cornelius Bliss, also hailed from a wealthy family yet started his career as a lowly clerk. He quickly learned to efficiently sell dry goods, particularly textiles and ready-to-wear clothing, and he eventually managed Bliss Fabyan & Co's New York City office and its large store in the middle of Manhattan's merchandise district. Known for his "clear mind and unquestioned force and probity of character," Bliss served as the long-term treasurer of the Republican National Committee, president of the American Protective Tariff League (working to make sure his firm did not have to compete against cheap textile imports), and Secretary of the Interior in the McKinley administration.[36] In 1900, Bliss turned down McKinley's invitation to run as his vice president. If not for that decision, he would have been president of the United States, which Theodore Roosevelt, who did accept the offer, became the following year when McKinley was assassinated.

The colonel's younger brother, Francis, followed the family's high-brow traditions and focused on its business. This "good son" was elected student body president at the Massachusetts Institute of Technology (and eventually became a trustee there), and after enjoying his post-graduation year "doing the grand tour of Europe," Francis returned home to become a partner at Bliss Fabyan & Co. Building on his father's example, he was elected director of several banks, including the New England Trust Company, led philanthropic efforts for the Boston's Free Hospital for Women, and joined prestigious social clubs. He also was his father's son in sports, sailing out of the Manchester Yacht Club and winning the prestigious Lipton Cup in both 1906 and 1907.

WANDERINGS

In contrast, George – the Fabyans' eldest son and the second of five children (born on March 15, 1867, just outside Boston) – rebelled against his well-connected family and its structured customs. An energetic youngster, he could not sit through formal dinners, and, although curious and bright, was bored by school and its rigid memorizations. He also had little patience for horses or boats, and his odd sense of humor tended to land him in trouble with both parents and teachers.

George's dealings with his stiff father were particularly strained. A bit rowdy and disheveled, he did not – and didn't want to – fit the family mold, and consistent comparisons to Francis only increased the tension. The difficult son, however, did absorb from George Francis the ability to make money and the enjoyment of science and horticulture.

Relations with his mother, the former Isabel Frances Littlefield, were more complicated. Although comfortable with – and proud of – her wealth and traditions, she appeared supportive of her rambunctious son, and George in later life would speak of his mother with great affection.

At the age of 16, George dropped out of school after only one year at Williston Seminary in East Hampton, Massachusetts. While he rejected the school's religious studies and its pressures to prepare for the ministry – concepts the lively youth found to be both stifling and boring – George was taken with the seminary's mantra of having each student "use what he has for the good of man."[37]

Preferring independence, George Fabyan severed relations with his father and mother, abandoned his substantial inheritance, and headed west. While his brother examined Europe's cathedrals and art museums, George roamed the American frontier, working for several years as a salesman for the Kirby Carpenter Company, a lumber merchant in Michigan, a tie and timber agent for the Union Pacific Railroad throughout the Northwest, and a cotton broker in Memphis, Tennessee.

The tall, muscular youth wandered throughout the West when it still was wild, wrangling with rugged men like himself and attracting an assortment of attractive women. Fabyan witnessed firsthand the western migration made possible by the railroads' vast expansion, soaring from 53,000 to almost 200,000 total rail miles in the 30 years after 1870. The lines linked the nation, with the Great Northern moving along the Canadian border, while the Southern Pacific connected New Orleans and Los Angeles, running across Texas and the Arizona and New Mexico territories. Those long-distance rails, as well as the hundreds of shorter lines throughout the industrial heartland, offered a vibrant means for Fabyan to market his ties and timber.

Trains also opened up western lands and markets. While the Homestead Act of 1862 is best known for providing 160 acres to anyone residing on property for five years, the rail companies, which received millions of acres in government subsidies, sold larger parcels to hundreds of families, providing access for those ranchers and farmers to customers in the East.

The railroads' rise impacted the Fabyan family in several direct and indirect ways. The lines, for instance, made it possible economically to transport throughout the country agricultural goods (such as cotton) and manufactured merchandise (such as cloth), providing a boon to Bliss Fabyan & Company. The consolidation of the rail companies also foreshadowed the era's numerous corporate mergers and the creation of giant trusts and powerful conglomerates. What Andrew Carnegie did with steel companies and John D. Rockefeller did with oil firms, Fabyan's father achieved, admittedly on a smaller scale, for cloth. These men were both hailed as captains of industry and lambasted as robber barons. Their very rise, in fact, prompted a government reaction, with the Supreme Court in 1886 allowing Washington to regulate interstate railroads, and Congress the following year approving the Interstate Commerce Act that ordered rail rates to be "reasonable."

The West's opportunities for a better life contributed to George Fabyan's can-do attitude. Contributing to the late 19th century's optimism was explosive technological innovation, with annual patents rising from fewer than 1,000 before the Civil War to more than 20,000 annually in the years from 1866 to 1900. Thomas Edison created a virtual factory for inventions at Menlo Park, New Jersey, an industrial research laboratory that inspired Fabyan. The prolific wizard and his technicians and machinists created an electric voting machine in 1869, a phonograph in 1877, the incandescent light bulb in 1879, the central electricity generator in 1882, and a motion picture projector in 1897. Edison, of course, was not the only inventor. Isaac Singer improved the sewing machine in 1843, George Westinghouse in 1868 developed railroad air brakes, Alexander Graham Bell devised the telephone in 1876, George Eastman created a hand camera in 1888, and others introduced the typewriter in 1867, barbed wire in 1874, and the adding machine in 1888. As these inventions came to market, they altered dramatically how Americans worked and played. The sewing machine and its industrial successors, moreover, enabled Bliss Fabyan & Company to more efficiently produce textiles and ready-to-wear garments, while the telegraph and telephone permitted instantaneous and direct communications, some of which the colonel understood needed to be encoded and kept secret.

Inventions and corporate conglomerates were not limited to heavy industry. Of particular benefit to the Fabyan cloth business, the late 19th century also witnessed the rise of large-scale retailing. John Wanamaker opened the first department store in 1876 in Philadelphia. That innovation – complete with heavy advertising and large-volume direct purchasing from manufacturers – was imitated by Rowland Hussey Macy in New York City and Marshall Field in Chicago. During this same period, Montgomery Ward and Julius Rosenwald created mail-order retail businesses targeted to those not living in major cities and their new department stores. Ward's 1872 catalog ran only a single page and listed nearly 150 items; by 1884, the directory exceeded 200 pages and 10,000 items.

Such technological and business advancements needed a justifying philosophy, which was provided by Andrew Carnegie, the Scottish immigrant who bought and managed steel smelters, railroads, steamships, and iron ore mines. His book, *Gospel of Wealth*, argued corporate competition insured the "survival of the fittest." While Carnegie admitted conglomerates

GEORGE FABYAN

widened the gap between rich and poor, he urged the wealthy to help others help themselves, and he set an example by building libraries, universities, and hospitals across the country. Fabyan felt a similar obligation, and he later would deploy his wealth to create a science center devoted to advancing research and bettering humanity.

On a scouting trip for railroad ties through Wisconsin's northern forests, George met Nelle Wright, a bright-eyed and energetic young lady who thought this inquisitive and handsome wanderer could take her away from tiny Walker. Theirs was an instant attraction, and they shared a desire for adventure and a sense of social purpose.

Nelle's father, Ely Wright, was a respected merchant who had run an Indian trading post when he was young. Although not a multimillionaire like George's father, Ely controlled a fair amount of wealth, allowing Nelle and her two brothers and two sisters to enjoy good schools and summer vacations at the family's lake house. Despite his affluence, Ely Wright was considered by acquaintances to be "a 'regular guy,' not an aristocrat."[38]

The couple married in 1890, George being 23 years old and Nelle almost six years his senior. Friends suggested Nelle offered a calming influence that prompted her husband to mature and mellow, at least a bit.

George and Nelle moved to Chicago, and he decided to rejoin the Fabyan family business – but on his own terms. Under an assumed name, George hired on as a warehouse assistant to Bliss Fabyan & Company's Midwest branch, where he worked hard and advanced. When the parent company's director – George's father – came to inspect the Chicago operations, the local foreman introduced the boss to this ambitious and successful young salesman. The reintroduction – the first meeting between father and son in almost a decade – allowed the black sheep to reclaim his inheritance, become the Midwest branch's resident partner, and obtain access to his family's business and political connections. Even Francis embraced the return of his prodigal brother, inviting George to be the best man at his June 1893 marriage in Boston's Old South Church.

WANDERINGS

George's western wanderings, particularly his time as a cotton broker in Tennessee and a timber trader in the West and Midwest, taught him the art of deal making, which proved most useful when he integrated back into Bliss Fabyan & Company. Yet this natural salesman also seemed to instinctively understand the nation's emerging urbanization created a ready market for ready-made clothes and textiles (e.g., sheets, curtains, and towels for new homes), and he grasped the best means to advertise those goods to the growing middle class. For instance, when the Bliss Fabyan mills produced a crinkled seersucker, he creatively labeled it "Ripplette" and marketed extensively, making the fabric – with puckered stripes separated from each other by stripes of flat, woven materials – the national standard for bedspreads and cotton goods.

Chapter 3
CHICAGO

George and Nelle moved to Chicago as Frederick Jackson Turner declared the American frontier closed. The recent census reported the nation's population density surpassed two persons per square mile, signifying the wilderness had been conquered and the country's vast lands had been settled. In Turner's paper, presented at the American Historical Association's convention in Chicago, the University of Wisconsin professor argued the now-vanished frontier had shaped the nation's past and molded a unique American character that featured individualism and inquisitiveness, qualities Colonel Fabyan displayed in abundance.

The couple also arrived in time for the 1893 Columbian Exposition, Chicago's elaborate celebration of progress and promise. The White City, designed by Daniel Burnham and landscaped by Frederick Law Olmsted, featured thousands of the newly introduced electric light bulbs that bedazzled appreciative crowds, and it introduced moving pictures, all-electric kitchens, long-distance telephones, zippers, Juicy Fruit gum, Cracker Jack candy, Melvil Dewey's (of Dewey Decimal System fame) vertical files, and many other wonders. The Fabyans and their new neighbors virtually swaggered throughout the park with confidence about the future.

GEORGE FABYAN

Burnham and Olmsted transformed what had been undeveloped marshes and sand dunes about seven miles south of the Loop into 600 acres of excitement. Seventy-two countries sent exhibits. Germany's Krupp Iron Works, for instance, displayed the world's largest gun, a canon nearly 60 feet long and able to propel shells 16 miles. Visitors virtually toured the world at the fairground's Algerian village, traditional Irish cottage, Cairo bazaar (complete with 175 Egyptians and a camel driver), and Buffalo Bill Cody's Wild West show (with 100 U.S. cavalry officers, 97 Indians, and sharpshooter Annie Oakley).

Superlatives reigned at the fair. The Manufacturers and Liberal Arts Building was the world's largest structure, covering 44 acres and able to accommodate 150,000 people. The Electricity Building glowed each evening with the largest collection – 130,000 – of electric light bulbs. The longest moving sidewalk transported visitors along a pier that stretched almost a half mile into Lake Michigan. A giant Ferris wheel rose a staggering 140 feet and carried 2,160 passengers at one time. Compared to the Philadelphia Exposition seven years before, the Chicago event attracted almost three times as many guests – more than 27 million.

The colonel was well positioned to take advantage of the city's optimism. Backed now by his family's wealth, he was a man with multiple interests and a drive for achievement. The handsome and athletic colonel also displayed a compelling charm and skilled salesmanship, able to market both cloths and ideas.

Business magnates, in fact, dominated Chicago at the turn of the 20th century. Joy Morton packaged salt and built a suburban estate and massive arboretum. Richard Sears, Julius Rosenwald, and Marshall Field marketed merchandise. William Wrigley introduced gum. George Pullman produced rail cars and built a model city for his employees. Samuel Insull delivered electricity and established a power empire throughout the Midwest. Francis Peabody mined coal. Philip Armour devised assembly-line slaughterhouses that each day butchered almost 13,000 hogs and 75,000 cattle. Cyrus McCormick manufactured the harvesters that revolutionized agriculture.

The cotton king mingled among these entrepreneurial giants. The colonel, in fact, convinced Pullman to use Fabyan's starched white sheets on the beds of his luxury railcars. He and Marshall Field, both broadly in the clothing business, regularly exchanged gifts and tales. Joy Morton visited Riverbank repeatedly to discuss trees, gardens, and his family.

Chicago tycoons tended to be self-made men. Unlike some of their New York counterparts who relied on fortunes left to them by fathers and grandfathers, rich midwesterners started from scratch or, like Fabyan, declared early independence and achieved some success on their own. Poet Carl Sandberg in 1916 captured that energy and gritty resolve by describing Chicago as "stormy, husky, brawling, City of the Big Shoulders. ... proud to be Hog Butcher, Tool Maker, Stacker of Wheat, Player with Railroads and Freight Handler to the Nation."

Yet the colonel stood apart from his Chicago colleagues. While they focused on their corporate empires, he preferred his laboratories to his downtown office, where he tended to stay only through lunch. While other tycoons turned to European gentry for architectural inspiration, Fabyan asked Frank Lloyd Wright, then a little-known architectural radical, to redesign his farm home in the modern "prairie" style. While they used their country estates to showcase their sophistication, the colonel created a working farm and sought credibility from his scientific achievements.

Beyond its corporate elite, Chicago's immigrant communities pulsed with chaotic dynamism when the Fabyans arrived. Reflecting the growing ethnic and religious amalgam, the city's Germans and Jews each published four native-language newspapers, while the Swedes and Poles maintained three each, with additional journals from the Norwegians, Danes, Bohemians, and Italians. The metropolis included the nation's largest Lutheran community and the second largest for Catholics and Jews, while more than 260,000 Chicagoans attended regular revivals by Dwight Moody, Billy Sunday, and other evangelical preachers.

GEORGE FABYAN

The Windy City's very appearance also seemed to be in motion, expanding both vertically and westward from Lake Michigan. Twenty-one years before the Fabyans joined this human mixture, a massive fire – the one allegedly sparked by Catherine O'Leary's cow – had destroyed 17,420 buildings, killed more than 300 people, and left almost 100,000 (of the city's 300,000) residents homeless. The burned-out downtown district measured about four miles long and one mile wide, yet the fire did not touch the stockyards, grain elevators, rail lines, and other key sources of Chicago's wealth.

Young and creative architects saw the destruction as an opportunity, and they utilized an array of new technologies – elevators, steel, interior lighting, and water pumps – to build higher and double the size of the business district. At ten stories, Chicago's Home Insurance Building, completed in 1884, became the nation's first skyscraper, and by the century's end the city's skyline featured numerous office buildings of 20 or more floors.

This Chicago School of Architecture became known worldwide for its steel framing, curtain walls, and large windows, as well as for its talented practitioners, including William Le Baron Jenney, Louis Sullivan, Martin Roche, and Daniel Burnham. Jenney synthesized much of the modern technology into the Leiter Building and the headquarters of the Home Insurance Company, yet it was Sullivan's massive and intricate Auditorium Building that remains the School's crowning achievement. In addition to its beauty, that structure – by providing a place where capitalists and workers, as well as various ethnic groups, could gather together to enjoy music – symbolized the era's struggle to calm the chaos associated with class and religious strife.

That strife was quite real and tempered the era's sense of progress. Laborers frequently walked off their jobs demanding better working conditions, while managers regularly ordered lockouts and hired Pinkerton detectives to beat back strikers. A particularly violent confrontation occurred on May 4, 1886, when thousands gathered in Chicago's Haymarket Square to support striking workers seeking an eight-hour day at the McCormick

Harvester factory. A steady rain gradually dispersed most of the crowd, leaving only about 300 to listen to the final speaker, when a squad of 150 policemen suddenly barged into the square and ordered everyone to leave. An unknown person threw a small dynamite bomb. Seven officers fell, prompting others to open fire into the crowd of protestors. The shooting spree lasted three long minutes and left a large number of workers dead.

Tensions accelerated in 1893, the year the Fabyans arrived, when the Pullman Palace Car Company cut wages, laid off workers, but did not lower rents or the prices of goods at its company-owned houses and stores. The American Railway Union, formed by Eugene V. Debs, responded by organizing some 3,000 Pullman workers to walk off their jobs and to refuse to advance any train that included a Pullman car, virtually stopping rail traffic throughout the Midwest and West.

Although Debs called for peaceful protests and Illinois Governor John Peter Altgeld sought a local solution, President Grover Cleveland in July 1894 ordered federal troops to Chicago, arguing the strikers were interfering with mail delivery and blocking interstate commerce. Commenting on the resulting violence and destruction, journalist Ray Stannard Baker wrote, "I saw long freight trains burning on side tracks. I saw Pullman cars that had been gutted by fire. I saw attacks by strikers on non-union men, and fierce conflicts between strikers and the police and deputies."[39] Overwhelmed by the military force, the union soon called off the strike, but Debs was jailed for violating a federal injunction. (Radicalized by the Pullman experience, Debs went on to found the Socialist Party and run five times for president, garnering more than 900,000 votes in 1912.)

The Panic of 1893 further tested Chicago's optimism. That four-year-long depression, the nation's worst economic crisis to date, caused unemployment to soar to 20 percent, scores of banks to close their doors, the prices of wheat and corn to fall dramatically, and the nation's gold reserves to be depleted. The federal government even had to plead for a loan from J. Pierpont Morgan and his banking syndicate in order to buy the 3.5 million ounces of gold required to satisfy the Treasury's need.

GEORGE FABYAN

Better than most Chicagoans, Fabyan weathered the financial downturn. Cloth sales remained stable, and the young executive continued to plan for expansion. The colonel's major setback was a temporary postponement of land purchases west of the city for an estate, farm, and laboratory.

In addition to the labor unrest and economic uncertainty, vice and corruption seemed to define Chicago at the turn of the century. Some 500 houses of prostitution – including the world-famous Everleigh – operated within the city limits as madams and pimps paid off policemen and politicians to look the other way. The Levee, a large red light area just south of the business center, became known as the nation's wickedest and wildest district. Aldermen, meanwhile, controlled political machines, and one bragged about placing 2,600 of his supporters on the public payroll.

Away from the Columbian Exposition's White City, Chicago also appeared dirty and polluted. Residents regularly dumped sewage and trash into the Chicago River, causing waterborne diseases, including dysentery and cholera, to kill an estimated 12 percent of the city's population in 1885. Another 1,009 died of typhoid in 1890, and an additional 2,000 succumbed the following year. A local newspaper editor described the river as "a mass of blood, grease, animal entrails, etc., the color being so dark as to be almost opaque when poured into a glass vessel."[40] Dark clouds of smoke, moreover, filled the air as Chicagoans burned dirty coal to heat their homes and power their factories.

Journalists and writers increasingly shone spotlights on this squalor. Upton Sinclair, for instance, portrayed in *The Jungle* the dismal working and sanitary conditions within the city's massive cattle yards and meatpacking plants. Lincoln Steffens attacked municipal corruption in *The Shame of the Cities* and declared Chicago (almost as a counterpoint to Carl Sandberg) to be "first in violence, deepest in dirt, loud, lawless, unlovely, ill-smelling, irreverent, new; an overgrown gawk of a village, the 'tough' among cities, a spectacle for the nation. Criminally it was wide open; commercially it was brazen; and socially it was thoughtless and raw."[41]

The strife, corruption, and filth motivated a new generation of reformers to bring justice and beauty to the urban scene. Daniel Burnham – the architect and designer who declared, "Make no little plans, they have no magic to stir men's blood" – created the map that organized Chicago's growth, centralized its cultural institutions in Grant Park along the lakefront, removed rail freight traffic from downtown, and created an outer ring of forest preserves. According to Burnham, "The time has come to bring order out of chaos incident to rapid growth, and especially the influx of people of many nationalities without common traditions or habits of life."[42]

Jane Addams, Mary McDowell, and Ellen Gates Starr, moreover, tried to temper the stresses facing working-class and immigrant families by offering affordable housing, public kindergartens, and libraries. Hull House, established in 1889 and located less than a mile from Chicago's downtown Loop, filled an entire city block with a dining hall providing inexpensive meals, a gymnasium and public playground offering recreation, and auditoriums featuring dance and music. Addams and her colleagues also gathered data on an array of urban challenges, created the field of social work, and advanced improvements in building codes, health care, and child labor laws.

A few of Chicago's elite supported the call for social order. Montgomery Ward, for instance, built bathing beaches beside Lake Michigan in order to provide peaceful escapes for the urban masses, and he orchestrated a campaign against haphazard development in order to keep Chicago's waterfront park "forever free and clear." The urban chaos, however, convinced several tycoons to escape west or north of the city. Francis Peabody, for instance, created his Mayslake estate in Oak Brook, while Fabyan in 1905 went a little further west to Geneva, on the banks of the Fox River, in order to build a retreat for scholarship.

World War I

Understanding Chicago – its tensions as well as its role in the world – helps inform the subsequent chapters that examine in more detail Fabyan's

GEORGE FABYAN

life and works. By 1914, foreign born and their children comprised 80 percent of the Windy City's population. When a Serbian nationalist shattered Europe's delicate alliances by assassinating Archduke Franz Ferdinand, heir to the throne of Austria-Hungary, ethnic tensions spilled onto Chicago's streets.

Czechs rallied against the Austro-Hungarian army's advances across their homeland, while Germans organized marches to support the Central Powers of Germany, Austria-Hungary, Bulgaria, and the Ottoman Empire (Turkey). Russian steelworkers, hostile to the czarist regime, held impromptu military drills, while Jewish immigrants from Eastern Europe cried out for Russia's defeat. Irish Americans found in the emerging war another reason to protest at British establishments.

The conductor of the Chicago Symphony Orchestra tried to straddle the strife by scheduling a medley of nationalistic songs during an outdoor concert at Ravinia, the outdoor music park just north of the city. Yet the French, Belgian, and Russian musicians refused to play "The Watch on the Rhine," while Germans, who made up the orchestra's majority, delivered sour notes during "Le Marseillaise," the French national anthem.

President Woodrow Wilson also tried to maintain neutrality, and he asked Americans to be "impartial in thought as well as in action." Yet neutrality proved difficult, particularly when German submarines in May 1915 sank the British ocean liner *Lusitania*, killing almost 1,200, including 128 Americans. Still, Wilson ran for reelection in 1916 on the slogan "He kept us out of war." The vote, however, was close, and the public's isolationism broke after British cryptographers deciphered the "Zimmerman telegram" that revealed Germany's secret plans to form an alliance with Mexico against the United States. Wilson pivoted quickly, declaring war was needed to make the world "safe for democracy," and he dispatched General John J. Pershing and the American Expeditionary Force to eastern France in June 1917.

George Fabyan welcomed the war. Having a clear enemy in his sights, the patriotic colonel dedicated Riverbank to training the nation's code crackers, improving the Navy's ability to detect German submarines, testing new mortars for trench warfare, and recruiting hundreds of soldiers. To do his part for home-front rationing, the colonel even built a windmill, planted wheat, and baked bread for his Geneva neighbors.

In contrast, Chicago's Germans, who had been the city's largest ethnic group, tried to lay low during the Great War. Frightened by jingoistic rallies and mobs defacing German statues and establishments, they canceled the annual German Day parade in 1916. Owners of the Bismarck Hotel renamed it Hotel Randolph, and the Kaiserhof Hotel became the Hotel Atlantic. The Chicago City Council even eliminated all Germanic street names, including Frankfurt, Rhine, and Berlin Avenues.

The conflict, by cutting off European immigration and increasing the demand for workers, brought benefits to Chicago's labor organizers and women. In order to guarantee steady supplies of equipment and food for the troops, the federal government forced plant managers to accept labor's demands for higher wages and improved benefits, allowing union memberships to rise substantially. The composition of the workforce also diversified as thousands of women took up jobs riveting tanks and airplanes.

At the same time, ever larger numbers of African Americans made their way north in search of jobs, doubling Chicago's black population during the 1910's, and those numbers continued to rise from less than 50,000 in 1910 to approximately 250,000 in 1930. The economic lure was compelling – tenant farmers or sharecroppers who had earned about $2 per week in the South obtained more than $2 per day when working in Chicago's immense stockyards.

The newly-arrived African Americans tended to settle in the South Side where the Stroll – a segment of State Street south of the Loop – became the center of jazz, culture, vibrancy, as well as gambling and drugs. Writer Langston Hughes described the Black Belt of 1918: "South State Street was in its glory then, a teeming Negro street with crowded theaters, restaurants, and cabarets. And excitement from noon to noon. Midnight was like day. The street was full of workers and gamblers, prostitutes and pimps, church folks and sinners."[43]

While a few African-American musicians played at downtown clubs – such as Louis Armstrong at the Blackhawk Restaurant – those facilities were closed to black customers, just as, increasingly, were housing opportunities outside of the Black Belt because white homeowners adopted restrictive covenants and refused to sell or rent to African Americans. To help ease the transition from southern farms to northern factories, Ida Wells-Barnet organized the Chicago-based Negro Fellowship League, which motivated the formation on a national level of the National Urban League. Racism, however, persisted in the city and throughout the North. With the arrival of the post-war recession, whites and blacks increasingly fought over scarce jobs and housing. Chicago's racial conflicts in the summer of 1919 killed 23 blacks and 15 whites, injured 537 others, and left a thousand homeless. The spark occurred on a hot, muggy afternoon at one of Lake Michigan's bathing beaches, which had been divided informally between whites and blacks. When a 17-year-old African American boy crossed the imaginary line as he drifted on a railroad tie in the slow current, several whites threw stones at him. The boy abandoned his float, tried to swim a few strokes, and drowned. Blacks angrily accused the whites of stoning him to death. Whites argued he had invaded their beach, much like they perceived black migrants had invaded their neighborhoods. Local newspapers described Chicago as being in a state of civil war for almost two weeks as blacks and whites alike were mobbed, beaten, and stabbed.

The post-war recession also increased unemployment, accelerated labor strife, and weakened organized unions. Stockyard employment fell by 15,000 during the first five months of 1919 and continued downward. In the steel industry that year, unions and their 18,000 workers tried to maintain wages and employment at the South Chicago smelters, yet they faced the massive U.S. Steel trust and a united coalition of smaller plants. Without government intervention, management held out, hired strikebreakers, and defeated the union. The Amalgamated Meat Cutters met a similar fate in 1921.

As if labor and racial conflict were not enough, Chicago suffered a major embarrassment in 1919 when the beloved White Sox, considered by some to be the greatest baseball team ever assembled, lost the World Series deliberately as part of a grand gambling scheme. Although a court failed to convict any ballplayers, the baseball commissioner, Chicago-based Judge Kenesaw Mountain Landis, banned eight athletes from the sport for life.

To escape the disappointments and chaos, Chicagoans took to theaters and roads. Movies and vaudeville shows attracted large crowds, including a weekly average of 46,000 at the ornate Chicago Theater on State Street; the colonel preferred the much smaller Arcada in Geneva, where he had a private box in the balcony's loge portion. Very few Americans could afford the expensive fleet of cars in Fabyan's garage, but motoring became increasingly popular, and by 1930 one of every eight Chicagoans owned an automobile. Throughout the 1920's, despite the shortage of paved roads, the number of cars soared from seven million to 23 million. Although Fabyan employed two chauffeurs, he enjoyed the personal freedom associated with getting behind the wheel, exiting his garage, and cruising along the Lincoln Highway.

Escaping with alcohol became more and more difficult as the war fervor of "no compromise" melded into the prohibition of beer and spirits, which were seen as diluting the nation's fighting efficiency. Some "patriots" saw prohibition as a means to target the German Americans who dominated the brewing and distillery industries, while progressives and evangelicals argued it would reduce crime and strengthen families. Building on the political organizing of the Anti-Saloon League, which sought to prohibit alcohol sales rather than just encourage individuals to stop drinking, Congress approved the 18th Amendment in 1917, and state legislatures ratified it rapidly, thereby banning the production, vending, and transportation of alcohol. Herbert Hoover called it "a great social and economic experiment, noble in motive and far-reaching in purpose."[44] Prohibition cut America's alcohol consumption in half during the 1920's, but it did not stop Fabyan and other tycoons from drinking cocktails and wines in their homes, and organized criminals found ways to bring beer and whiskey to the masses at speakeasies and social clubs.

Alphonse Capone arrived in 1921 to help satisfy Chicago's illegal thirst, and, in the process, advanced the city's reputation as the nation's gangster and murder capital. The 21-year-old was lured from Brooklyn's Five Points gang to help control Johnny Torrio's growing empire of brothels, saloons, and gambling houses. After two years of pimping and overseeing several houses of prostitution, Capone became manager of the Four Deuces club in the old Levee District, and, by the age of 25, he was overseeing much of Chicago's underworld and bringing in annual profits of about 40 million in today's dollars. Although he portrayed himself as a second-hand furniture dealer, the new boss of the "Outfit" created a sophisticated business by taking advantage of the Thompson submachine gun, automobile, telephone, and other new technologies.

At least a dozen bootlegging gangs divided up the city in the early 1920's. Most bribed local officials and law enforcement officers in order to transact business. The Genna Gang in the Little Italy neighborhood, for instance, paid $500 monthly to police captains and up to $125 to beat cops. According to the city's police chief, 60 percent of his officers were involved in the bootlegging business.[45]

Capone eventually abandoned the coexistence policy of his mentor Torrio and launched a virtual war against the O'Banion syndicate, then run by Bugs Moran. More than 500 gang murders shocked Chicago, with the most notorious killings on St. Valentine's Day in 1929 when Capone had hired out-of-town hit men, who, after stealing a police car and uniforms, entered a warehouse on North Clark Street that Moran used to distribute liquor and beer. The pretend police lined up seven of Moran's gang against the wall and shot them repeatedly. One bootlegger, who survived for a few hours, suffered 22 bullet wounds.

Capone subsequently gained control of alcohol sales to Chicago's 10,000 speakeasies, as well as liquor supply sources from the Caribbean to Canada. By 1930, his business's annual income exceeded $70 million (almost $900 million in today's dollars). He employed more than 700 well-armed men, some of whom traveled in front and behind his armored car as it cruised Chicago's streets. Capone also enjoyed the city's many theaters and jazz clubs and showed up regularly with 18 henchmen hiding guns beneath their coats.

The boss used his substantial muscle and profits to play in the political world. He essentially controlled the local government in Cicero, home of the massive Western Union manufacturing plant, and in 1927, he financed Republican Big Bill Thompson's return to Chicago's city hall in an election that featured stolen ballot boxes and bombings of Democratic offices.

Roaring into Depression

The 1920's were good years economically for Capone, Fabyan, and most Chicagoans. Manufacturing production rose, a growing middle class moved to the suburbs, stock prices soared, and business barons partied. Few, however, noticed inflation was rising and speculative broker loans had almost doubled in the previous two years.

On one level, the 1920's were known for their "roar," flapper fashions, jazz concerts, and Charleston dance crazes. Yet the nation and the city turned quite conservative when World War I ended. Following Warren Harding's call for "a return to normalcy," Americans abandoned the Progressive Era's reforming zeal as well as the Democrat's call for international moral leadership and a League of Nations. Despite economic prosperity on the home front, hate groups, such as the Ku Klux Klan, flourished by stoking fear of blacks and foreigners. The influence of Protestant fundamentalists also rose as preachers railed against Catholicism, alcohol, evolution, jazz, and rising hemlines. The World Christian Fundamentalist Union, for instance, hired William Jennings Bryan, a three-time presidential candidate, to argue against the public school teaching of Darwin's theories on evolution in the so-called "monkey trial" that was broadcast to the nation over radio.

GEORGE FABYAN

A series of three Republicans – Harding, Calvin Coolidge, and Herbert Hoover – controlled the White House throughout the 1920's and they backed away from government regulations; lowered taxes, particularly on the wealthy; cut federal spending; and raised tariffs in order to protect U.S.-based corporations (something advanced by Cornelius Bliss, George Francis Fabyan's business partner). Coolidge epitomized the era's political perspective with his quip "The business of America is business."

Lax regulation led to several scandals. The most egregious – focused on the Navy's oil reserves at Teapot Dome, Wyoming, and Elk Hills, California – was exposed by Fabyan and the Friedmans, who, as will be explained below, cracked the coded messages that proved Albert Fall, Harding's Interior Secretary, had received no-interest "loans" in exchange for secretly steering public-land leases to private petroleum companies controlled by Harry Sinclair and Edward Doheny. Fall resigned under pressure, the first cabinet minister to do so, and then was convicted of bribery.

The era's economic prosperity did not extend to farmers. When the armistice agreement reduced the demand for corn and wheat, commodity prices fell. The rural community's response was to plant more crops, but the resulting overproduction led to even further price cuts and economic misery on farms.

Still, for most urban and suburban Americans, the 1920's offered higher wages and lower prices. With living standards improving, consumption soared and Fabyan's friend Marshall Field and other retailers sold thousands of new appliances and gadgets, including washing machines, refrigerators, vacuums, and electric razors, all of which allowed Samuel Insull to expand his electricity empire. Field's main store at State and Washington Streets, a palatial emporium that one shopper described as "fairly land," marketed sophistication and glamour to Chicago's women who enjoyed their families' higher incomes. It was Nelle Fabyan's favorite store, and she was driven there for a day of shopping at least once a month with her sisters or friends.

Radio broadcasts, which the Sabines at Riverbank helped perfect, fired that consumerism with advertisements claiming new cars and appliances would bring to Americans elegance, youth, and love. The first commercial radio station opened in Pittsburgh in 1920, broadcasting the presidential election results, and the number of homes with receivers rose from 60,000 in 1922 to more than ten million in 1929. Beginning in 1926 with the National Broadcasting Company (NBC), many local radio stations joined together to form coast-to-coast networks.

Culture, in many respects, became nationalized during the 1920's. Motion pictures, again with the assistance of Fabyan and the Sabines, were shown across the country, and their celebrities – such as Mary Pickford, who visited the colonel at Riverbank – were transformed into popular icons that became the grist for tabloid newspapers and magazines, such as *Time*, which Henry Luce launched in 1923. The exploits of sports heroes, including baseball's Babe Ruth and boxing's Jack Dempsey, similarly were followed by millions throughout the nation. In 1921, *Reader's Digest* began offering condensed versions of magazine articles and books, and in 1926, the Book-of-the-Month Club introduced steep discounts for publications the editors felt all Americans should read.

Chicago's Samuel Insull epitomized the era's hopes and risks. Thomas Edison's former secretary took over the struggling Chicago Edison Company in 1892 and quickly raised money, including $250,000 from Marshall Field, to build new power plants and buy out his numerous competitors. His electric empire eventually served more than 4 million customers in 32 states and produced one-eighth of the nation's power.

Insull's corporate pyramiding pleased investors, who drove up the price of Insull Utility Investments from $12 to $570 a share. According to one calculation, the company's value "appreciated at an around-the-clock rate of $7,000 per minute, for a total rise of more than one-half billion dollars."[46]

Yet such exponential expansion could not continue, and the stock rally broke in early September 1929. Although the market quickly recovered, evidence mounted that the good times of the Roaring 20's had been based on a shaky pyramid of debt. Economists began to notice business inventories were rising as consumer spending was shrinking, and the Federal Reserve Board recently raised interest rates to curb speculation, yet most investors ignored the warnings and banks persisted with risky loans. No one, however, could ignore the "perfect Niagara of liquidation" that occurred in October 1929, particularly on the 24th, known as Black Tuesday. It was, said historian Frederick Lewis Allen, "the dumping on the market of hundreds of thousands of shares of stock held in the name of miserable traders whose margins were exhausted or about to be exhausted."[47]

Insull's highly leveraged utility business could not survive the run of bad news. His is H holding companies – which had soared because of fragile pyramiding, inflated assets, and questionable accounting – withered under the financial strain. The value of his securities plummeted $150 million in one week, with a share of his stock eventually falling from $570 to only $1.25.

A federal official labeled Insull's financial fallout as "the tragedy of the century." Describing the individual investor's plight, he said, "One day I stood and watched those holding securities and obligations of these companies coming in and filing them (to receive a refund.) They were just the average run of people – clerks and schoolteachers there in Chicago, small shopkeepers in Illinois, farmers from Wisconsin – and what they brought in, of course, was worth nothing. They had lost every penny."[48]

The Great Depression left more than 33 million Americans (about a quarter of the labor force) without jobs, yet its impact was particularly pronounced in Chicago, where the unemployment rate reached an unprecedented 40 percent by 1932. Almost 50 percent of the city's blacks had no job. Only half the workers at manufacturing plants in 1927 were employed by 1933, and the city's industrial output fell more than 60 percent.

Property values plummeted and evictions soared. Some 300,000 Chicagoans were forced to live in a so-called Hooverville near an old garbage dump at 31st and Cicero, while another 1,500 slept along the lower level of the Michigan Avenue bridge. Just 51 of the city's 228 mortgage-lending banks remained open by September 1931.

Chicago's school teachers missed 24 pay checks, prompting more than 14,000 instructors to storm downtown banks in late 1934 and demand their suspended salaries.[49] On Labor Day 1931, some 40,000 unionists marched down Michigan Avenue calling for jobs. In January of the following year, 300 men and women battled police at the Abraham Lincoln Center when the government's rent relief ran out, and riots regularly broke out in neighborhoods when officials tried to evict renters behind on their payments. Unemployment appeals rose by almost 600 each day, even though assistance funds had all but vanished. The mayor appealed for federal help by telling lawmakers their only choice was to either send money or dispatch troops.

The Depression certainly hit hardest on the poor, but even Fabyan and his millionaire colleagues felt the pinch. Bliss Fabyan & Company was forced to restructure in the early 1930's, and George and his brother Francis subsequently retired from day-to-day operations. The colonel tried to keep up appearances by continuing to entertain guests, yet he trimmed expenses and fervently sought corporate clients and government contracts to cover Riverbank's acoustical testing and cryptographic research. Although he paid his own workers little, Fabyan did demonstrate charity, frequently arranging for Geneva grocers to provide food to poor families as well as creating make-work projects at his estate that gave jobs to the unemployed.

Immigrants

Chicago in the early 20th century – with its vast factories, steel mills, and packinghouses – served as a magnet for immigrant job seekers, particularly from eastern and southern Europe. Poles, Czechs, Lithuanians, Russians, Jews, and Germans settled in segregated neighborhoods and created their own ethnic schools, churches, clubs, and newspapers.

Fabyan certainly hired numerous immigrants to clean his villa and tend his gardens, but he had moved west in part to evade Chicago's ethnic chaos. He also avoided most of the city's raucous political debates, but even this conservative patriot became increasingly frustrated with the corruption and cronyism practiced by the long-time Republican leaders.

It was immigrants, however, who changed Chicago's governance. New ethnic politicians, such as Anton Cermak, began to build a Democratic machine at the same time the Depression weakened the Republicans' traditional support from white, American-born voters.

Czech-born Cermak entered the Illinois General Assembly in 1902 at the age of 29. From his base in the Lower West Side, he built what one historian described as "a masterful coalition that included groups previously outside of the party structure."[50] He brokered deals among the ethnic wards and labor unions in order to create a powerful political machine. Capitalizing on the pro-drinking sentiments of German, Irish, and other ethnic communities, Cermak increasingly targeted prohibition. Several Chicago precincts had voted themselves dry, largely as an anti-immigrant measure, yet the up-and-coming politician sided with the "wets" and soon was elected president of the fast-growing United Societies for Local Self Government.

In the mayoral race of 1931, Cermak also had the advantage of running against the scandal-prone and clownish Republican mayor, Big Jim Thompson, whose antics included riding a horse onto the Cort Theater during a campaign rally and parading through Chicago's streets in his Stetson hat and cowboy boots with various animals that were to symbolize and mock his political opponents. Thompson referred to Cermak as a "Bozo" and a "Bohunk." Voters, however, had grown weary of the vaudeville and, more importantly, of Thompson's ties to Al Capone and organized crime. Just before the election, in fact, the states attorney raided the offices of a Thompson appointee, who also was a known Capone associate. Even groups of Republican women supported Cermak as the best means to weed out corruption from City Hall, and the *Chicago Tribune* endorsed the Democrat and his promise for a "New Deal" for the city. The local newspaper went so far as to state, "For Chicago, Thompson has meant filth, corruption, obscenity, idiocy, and bankruptcy. ... He has given the city an international reputation for moronic buffoonery, barbaric crime, triumphant hoodlumism, unchecked graft, and a dejected citizenship."[51]

Chicago's first immigrant mayor won by a substantial 191,916 votes. One year later, Cermak mobilized his diverse Democratic coalition, inserted the ethnically-popular "Wetest of the Wet" plank into the national party's platform, and delivered the city and the state for Franklin Roosevelt, who promised a "New Deal" for the entire county.

While a gifted manager of his political machine, Cermak, according to one commentator, was "not a very nice man."[52] Another described him as "rough and intimidating ... with few social graces."[53] Yet he achieved almost mechanical efficiency in the operation of city services and set the model for political patronage.

Responding to pleas by Cermak and other urban politicians, President Franklin Roosevelt experimented repeatedly in order to revive the nation's depressed economy. During his first 100 days in the White House, the new chief executive pushed through the Emergency Banking Reform Act and established the Federal Deposit Insurance Corporation, the Civilian Conservation Corps, and the Tennessee Valley Authority (TVA). The short-term results were mixed. Gross national product rose slightly, yet more than ten million Americans remained unemployed.

The New Deal, however, clearly delivered for Chicago. The Works Progress Administration brought 40,000 jobs to the city, most of which were controlled by Cermak's political operation. Federal support, in fact, allowed Chicago to lay the 17-mile-long Outer Drive (later renamed Lake Shore Drive) along Lake Michigan, to dig the State Street subway, to construct 30 new public schools, to build the first three public housing projects, to enlarge Midway Airport, and to landscape Lincoln and several other parks.[54]

Cermak, tragically, did not get to celebrate the completion of those various projects. In February 1933, the mayor had traveled to Florida to visit the new president. After FDR delivered a short speech and his car began to leave Miami's Bayfront Park, shots rang out. Cermak and four

GEORGE FABYAN

others fell. Roosevelt directed his vehicle to the bloodied mayor, whom he cradled as the motorcade sped to the hospital. Cermak is said to have told the president, "I'm glad it was me instead of you." He struggled for 19 days but died on March 6. According to historian Dominic Pacyga, "The martyred mayor's funeral included thirty thousand marchers, while twenty-three thousand attended ceremonies at the Chicago Stadium, and fifty thousand witnessed his burial at the Bohemian National Cemetery in near zero temperatures."[55]

While Chicago changed dramatically in the early 20th century, Fabyan was changing the world. The city's dynamism certainly inspired the colonel, and the periods of economic expansion allowed his cloth business to flourish, which, in turn, enabled him to hire more and more researchers who he motivated with the vision, enthusiasm, and resources needed to help synchronize sound, end a world war, and make cryptography a science.

GEORGE FABYAN

George and Nelle Fabyan
(Friends of Fabyan)

George Fabyan
(George C. Marshall Foundation,
Lexington, VA)

Elizebeth Friedman
and George Fabyan
(George C. Marshall Foundation,
Lexington, VA)

Nelle Fabyan
(Friends of Fabyan)

43

GEORGE FABYAN

Riverbank students spelling out "Knowledge is Power"
(George C. Marshall Foundation, Lexington, VA)

Elizebeth and William Friendman
(George C. Marshall Foundation,
Lexington, VA)

Elizabeth Wells Gallup

GEORGE FABYAN

Wallace Sabine

Paul Sabine

Riverbank Villa and Hell Chair
(Kathryn Tandy)

Engineering Building
(Kathryn Tandy)

GEORGE FABYAN

Fabyan Windmill
(Kathryn Tandy)

Riverbank Gardens, Lighthouse, and Windmill
(George C. Marshall Foundation, Lexington, VA)

Chapter 4
RIVERBANK

Some 40 miles to the west of Chicago lies Geneva, a village along the Fox River. Less than a mile downstream in the early 20th century were a few farmhouses and fields that George Fabyan would mold into a separate world.

Riverbank, in fact, became Fabyan. The estate and laboratories were his life's work, and he oversaw virtually every aspect of their design and operation. The lavish gardens, unique architecture, and zoo displayed his wacky and creative ways, while the think tank influenced world events and made the colonel seem larger than life.

The colonel ruled the diverse estate almost as a feudal lord. Cigarette in hand, he walked the grounds, at least once a day, delivering orders in his low gruff voice. When not supervising the gardeners and field hands, he spent most of his time asking questions of his "community of thinkers," whom, he argued, were conducting "remarkable and humanitarian research work."[56]

About a dozen years after moving to Chicago, Fabyan began buying land along the Fox River. He purchased his first ten acres, what had been the Joel Harvey farm, in 1905. Up until 1936, he regularly added additional tracts, ranging from ten to 113 acres, until the estate totaled some 350 acres. Route 31, which became the Lincoln Highway, divided the property, with the laboratories and several houses and dormitories on the west side, while across the road sat the villa, Japanese garden, garage, greenhouses, animal cages, and boat house. The island halfway across the Fox River featured Fabyan's lighthouse and Roman swimming pool, while the eastern bank eventually included agricultural fields, a distinctive Dutch windmill, and the colonel's "gallery of junk." The property was so large it included three trolley stops on the line operated by the Aurora-Elgin & Fox River Electric Company.

While the colonel continued to expand the Bliss Fabyan & Company, where he proved to be a natural salesman, he focused most of his substantial energies on managing Riverbank and the 150 workers employed within the labs, villa, gardens, and farm. Twenty-five gardeners, for instance, tended the flowers, which wife Nelle arranged into colorful bouquets, some of which were sent by train daily to Chicago hotels and restaurants.

Riverbank, according to a leading Chicago newspaper, was "one of the strangest and, at the same time, most beautiful country estates in America."[57] Workers found it to be a lovely, almost luxurious, place to live and work. Fabyan's Swedish servants ensured the researchers were, in the words of one, "treated like barons." Although the colonel paid them little, "hardly enough to buy lunches," they enjoyed lavish meals and wine at the lodge and dining halls, as well as fresh flowers and fruit in their offices and rooms.

The Fabyan estate also offered a wonderland for the children of Riverbank employees. "Back in the early days the place was quite a showcase," said Don Williams, whose mother had been a cook to the Fabyans. "It was really something to be a kid growing up in a place like that."[58] John Butler, whose father was a chauffeur and who himself worked at Riverbank Laboratories for 35 years, recalled his early years: "It was real nice to live there. I had access to boats and animals and the pools."[59]

Fabyan relished giving tours, particularly for visiting academics. Upon completing the circuit around Riverbank's gardens and fields, he would return to the laboratories, beat his chest, and boast about how a high school dropout had created a world-class research institute. The colonel was particularly proud of his Engineering Building, which he designed after collecting hundreds of 15-foot steel I-beams that went unclaimed in a Chicago rail yard. Initially, the colonel simply told the contractor to build a garage that would use every one of the I-beams, but the builder demanded some sort of design. Fabyan responded by stacking cigarette tins against his office wall and declaring each box represented a 15-by-15-foot room. The fifth and highest floor featured a single such room that became Fabyan's reflection chamber, where he could close behind him a trap-door entrance and ensure privacy. From the east, the building appeared to be a boxy pyramid, while straight overhangs on each floor punctuated the western wall.

The colonel hid his own office in the back of the structure, requiring visitors to pass through a massive vault door, take numerous turns, and squeeze down narrow hallways. The room's west wall featured more of Fabyan's junk collection, this time dozens of sailing-ship portholes as well as segments of a lighthouse lamp. The office's key fixture, however, was the colonel's grand wooden desk, which he assembled first and then constructed walls around it.

The adjacent office housed Adele Cumming, Riverbank's real manager. Known as Belle, this "perfectionist and ardent task master" supervised the estate's staff, accounted for the finances in meticulous black folders, and provided order to the colonel and his diverse ventures. Born in Inverness, Scotland, she was able to intimidate visitor and staff alike, and she was the only Riverbank employee able to stand up to the colonel's feared "bellowing." Said one employee, "Hands on hips, her eyes narrowed in a stern, disapproving look, she was able to cow even the most stalwart of guests."[60] Belle also was noted for her foul mouth, something that particularly irritated the religious Paul Sabine, who repeatedly asked her to refrain. After a week of swearing abstinence, Belle asked the sound expert if he noticed any difference. When Sabine said "No," she swore loudly, to which he replied, "See."[61] This drill sergeant, however, orchestrated a sense of community among the Riverbank staff, frequently writing postcard greetings and purchasing small gifts for the chauffeurs and researchers. Moreover, she was beloved by Fabyan, who invited her (and virtually no other staffer) to afternoon teas at the villa.

Down the hall from the offices, on the other side of the vault door, stood the laboratory for fire-retardant experiments, where engineers directed gas flames at various test materials until they bubbled and burned. A separate room was devoted to physiology and anatomy, particularly problems associated with bodily balance. According to one of Fabyan's scientists, it included "appliances to be used in correction and reeducation of physical maladjustments, including electrical appliances for experimentation in muscle action."[62]

Yet another lab featured radiation experiments and cancer research, made possible by three-quarters of a million dollars worth of radium stored in a lead-lined radioactive box. The X-ray testing, particularly the images of girls standing behind radiation-ray screens, led *Scientific American* to declare: "The (Riverbank) scientists, pegging away at the secrets of nature, sooner or later break down existing barriers, open the way to a new field, and we are soon confronted with brand new opportunities for exploration."[63]

Riverbank's X-ray experiments led to other, less upbeat, tales. Fabyan, it was said by associates, collected from Chicago hospitals and cemeteries numerous unclaimed cadavers that his scientists would radiate, cut, probe, and dissect, and then bury the remains in secret graves around the estate. According to one researcher, "The Geneva police would be shocked if they ever started digging up the back yard." With a sly smile, he added, "Johnny Putrid is buried out there somewhere."[64]

Such laboratory practices prompted numerous ghost stories, and several employees feared working late when the building's beams would creak and chairs would seem to move. Some recalled looking out the windows into the dark yard and seeing running girls with flowing white trains. (Another dismissed these visions as nothing more than the "bad girls" from the nearby reform school on evening jaunts.) After Fabyan's death, a few staffers claimed sightings of the colonel's phantom.

Some real mysteries, however, remain about this Engineering Building. On the western side of the second floor were some 200 phone outlets, and the archives include pictures of scores of women on telephones, either standing or sitting on benches along the wall. Some current employees guess Fabyan ran a stock brokerage, while others suggest a bookie operation.

Just to the south of the engineering complex, on the other side of a small walkway, stands the Acoustics Laboratory, completed in 1918 and costing Fabyan almost $1.1 million in today's dollars. It was the world's first lab for the exclusive study of acoustics, and is still considered one of the best.

This building's exterior featured Fabyan's quirky and hodgepodge tastes, including a six-story bell tower in one corner topped with a massive sculpture of a golden eagle. One design critic referred to the structure as "architectural dementia."[65]

The tower's bell – measuring 36 inches at its base and 29 inches tall – struck a series of perfect "A's" at the start of every work day, at lunch break, and at quitting time. On each of those occasions, the colonel ordered the bell to ring a set number of times. At his death in 1936, that number was cut in half, and the bell was silenced when Nelle Fabyan passed away in 1939.

The structure's interior reverberation chamber, essentially a room within a room, was designed by Wallace Sabine, the distinguished Harvard physicist, and included a two-foot gap between the exterior and interior walls that provided a sound-proof barrier for acoustical experiments and testing. Fabyan named the structure for the scientist and dedicated it to Sir Francis Bacon's dictim: "Knowledge is power," which he inscribed above the main entrance.

The acoustics chamber tested the sound-absorbing properties of numerous materials, yet tuning forks remained the laboratory's consistent focus and product. Originally used to harmonize a levitation machine's strings, the forks were refined to answer Nelle's off-handed question about whether the British or the Americans made better bells. (The answer, concluded the diplomatic colonel, was the bells were of equal quality.) Riverbank's sophisticated tuning forks, as noted above, allowed the Associated Press to synchronize its senders and receivers in order to transmit photographs long distance. The tuning-fork business – now known as Riverbank Acoustical Laboratories and owned by Alion Science and Technology – moved recently to downtown Geneva and continues to produce world-class forks used for a variety of purposes, from harmonizing pianos to calibrating police radar guns.

Also on the west side of Route 31 were Riverbank's guest houses, dormitories, and a U-shaped complex of adjoining buildings, the largest of which was known as "The Grille." The lower level of that two-story unit served as the estate's main dining hall, while the upper floor contained private rooms and bunk beds for unmarried workers.

The research campus's main lodge, which provided offices for Mrs. Elizabeth Gallup and her cryptographic assistants, was Fabyan's initial architectural design project, with the broad and recessed porch, multi-paned windows, and open gables being inspired by an article within the March 1909 edition of *The Craftsman* entitled "A Roomy, Homelike Farmhouse for Lovers of Plain and Wholesome Country Life." While Fabyan could not easily be classified as "plain" or "wholesome," the structure's style reflected his rejection of the era's industrial materials and high-style excesses in favor of simplicity and human-scale harmony with the environment.

Route 31 divided the colonel's property and became part of the Lincoln Highway, the nation's first coast-to-coast road. Unlike today's interstates, the highway was a compilation of existing two-lane trails that wandered through 13 states, over 3,389 miles, from Times Square in New York City to Lincoln Park in San Francisco.

In the early 1910's, less than 9 percent of America's rural roads featured "improved" surfaces of gravel, brick, shells, or oiled earth. Most were composed of simple dirt that turned into muddy bogs after a storm or dust bowls during droughts. Carl Fisher, an early automotive entrepreneur who manufactured the Prest-O-Lite carbide-gas headlights used on most early vehicles, believed his business – and the American economy – would boom only if cars and trucks had good roads on which to move. A skilled promoter, Fisher also created the Indianapolis Motor Speedway in order to highlight fast and sleek automobiles, and he gathered industry leaders in September 1912 to pledge $1 million for a coast-to-coast rock highway that would be completed by May 1915, in time for San Francisco's Panama-Pacific International Exposition. Thomas Edison, President Woodrow Wilson, and former President Theodore Roosevelt opened their wallets, but Henry Ford, then the largest auto maker, refused, arguing the government, not businesses or individuals, should build America's roads.

Fisher and his friends formed the Lincoln Highway Association "to procure the establishment of a continuous improved highway from the Atlantic to the Pacific, open to lawful traffic of all descriptions without toll charges." Fisher hoped the highway would serve as an example and "stimulate as nothing else could the building of enduring highways everywhere that will not only be a credit to the American people but that will also mean much to American agriculture and American commerce."[66]

The Lincoln Highway Association launched a "Trail Blazer" tour to scout the route, and its members were lobbied by local officials wanting their towns to gain the economic benefits of being on the new interstate. Mayors of Geneva, Batavia, and St. Charles organized enthusiastic rallies to demonstrate the benefits of a route along the western bank of the Fox River. Fabyan became a fervent supporter for he realized an improved road would allow him to attract more guests, to move his farm products to markets, as well as to enjoy weekend journeys in his Rolls Royce.

This so-called "Main Street Across America" was dedicated in late October 1913 and quickly brought prosperity and freedom of movement to Geneva and hundreds of towns across the country. It inspired several other long-distance roads, such as the Dixie Highway and the Yellowstone

GEORGE FABYAN

Trail, and it motivated Dwight Eisenhower, then a young soldier crossing the country on an Army convoy, to later champion as president the National Interstate and Defense Highways Act of 1956.

Across Route 31 from the Riverbank laboratories stood the Fabyan villa. Although substantial in size, it was no European-styled mansion in the model of other Chicago millionaires. In fact, Fabyan initially purchased a rather simple farm house, but in 1907 hired Frank Lloyd Wright to add features that would complement the surrounding prairie. Two of Fabyan's neighbors – the Gridleys of Batavia and the Hoyts of Geneva – had previously employed Wright, and the colonel appreciated the architect's confidence and flair, as well as his interest in Japanese art and culture. Wright was still relatively unknown, although his innovative (some would say "radical") work on the Larkin Building in Buffalo, New York, had won broad attention.

The architect, who periodically traveled by train the 30 miles from his home in Oak Park in order to supervise the Riverbank construction, added three verandas, a south wing, and peaked casement windows with large overhangs – transforming what had been an L-shaped structure into one that, from above, took on the form of a cross. The new features stressed the horizontal, a key feature of Wright's style, and a restoration specialist described the Fabyan villa as "special and inspired" and as "one of Wright's last great gable buildings."[67] Speaking of the architect's work at Riverbank, the critic also commented, "The roof of the Fabyan Villa is very strong. It's some of the most powerful roof geometry I've seen (Wright) do for this period."[68]

Fabyan and Wright, both strong-willed individuals, argued often about the structure's style and contents. During one heated conversation, the colonel summarily fired the architect, although tempers eventually cooled, in good part because of Nelle's diplomatic influence, and they continued the joint project. Wright was notorious for dictating interior colors and furniture designs, and he installed his signature built-in benches, five-sided windows, and wood banding throughout. Yet the colonel, no slouch in getting his own way, ensured his villa would be the only Wright house with a stuffed bear and three mounted buffalo in the living room. Not liking furniture legs – since they could break and, even when they didn't, conveyed an unwelcomed sense of immobility – Fabyan also arranged for a three-seated couch, divans, and beds to swing from ceiling beams on thick chains. The colonel, again over Wright's objections, also built exterior compartments to hold the large logs that fueled his beloved fireplaces and fire pits.

Despite their disagreements and arguments, the two individualists clicked. Fabyan's employing the controversial architect, in fact, reflected the tycoon's willingness to engage a field's best and brightest. Wright, meanwhile, sought out wealthy men with interests in technology and the ability to think progressively. Describing his clients, the architect said, "I found them chiefly among American men of business with unspoiled instincts and untainted ideals. A man of this type usually has the faculty of judging for himself."[69] The two men, coincidently, were born in the same year, 1867, and each left school before graduating in order to pursue his wanderlust and passion.

Fabyan valued Wright's work enough to hire him subsequently to remodel the Fox River Country Club, just down the road from the villa. The architect added to the Victorian structure a 30-foot-by-75-foot north wing, along the outside of which he installed a broad porch protected by a deep over-hanging roof. The addition's upper level featured a dance/banquet/dining hall, while the lower floor included billiard tables and a bowling alley. Unfortunately, the structure, considered by the local newspaper to be "one of the most handsome buildings in the Fox River valley," burned to the ground just three years after it was redesigned, leaving just two charred fireplace chimneys.

Nelle's bedroom was on the Riverbank villa's first floor, where her bed hung from the ceiling by four cables and her adjacent bathroom featured a special shower in which semi-circular tubes with spray holes were stacked

GEORGE FABYAN

about six inches apart. An avid collector, Nelle populated her room with stuffed birds and small animals native to Northern Illinois, as well as an extensive collection of porcelain and glazed terra cotta figurines. One of her favorite pieces was a fat and toothless Oriental man sitting atop a pigeon-toed turtle.

The colonel occupied the entire second floor, and his two bedrooms received sunlight on three sides from diamond-shaped windows within deep-set gables. His bathroom was as large as the downstairs dining room.[70]

The Fabyans' sleeping arrangement – separate rooms on separate floors – was not uncommon for the era but illustrated the couple's rather unique relationship. No doubt the two displayed tenderness and mutual support, but Nelle's inability to bear children and George's desire for privacy reduced their opportunities for intimacy.

In fact, George paid females to provide him an heir to whom he could leave Riverbank and carry-on his family name. One surrogate mother, despite Fabyan's payments, refused at the hospital to give up her newborn, and another's baby died at birth. While at the hospital tending to that woman, the colonel offered to "buy" the baby girl from the woman in the next bed who was struggling to raise six other children. In the midst of an economic recession, that mother considered for several days the colonel's offer of wealth and education, but in the end she couldn't abandon her daughter.

In 1984, that daughter, then middle aged, arrived unannounced at Riverbank to ask if the villa was where Miss X (who had been the colonel's mistress) had lived. The laboratory's shocked manager remembered Fabyan's activities, and the daughter offered her story: "You see, my mother was in the hospital having me and she shared the room with Miss X, who had just had a miscarriage. My mother has told the story many times about the wealthy colonel who had offered a lot of money for me. So while growing up, my mother and I often discussed the fact that I could have been very rich as the colonel's daughter but the love my mother and I shared could never have been equaled. Of course, there were many times I recall daydreaming of living the life of a wealthy heiress at Riverbank. You see, we were very poor."[71]

Fascinated with modern devices, Fabyan installed a signaling system in each room of the house that rang in the butler's pantry. The master control panel, considered quite advanced for its day, featured lights for each area, allowing staff to quickly respond to the Fabyans' requests.

The colonel also installed a great electric organ he could operate automatically or play on the keyboard. Fabyan activated the instrument most evenings, attracting a great deal of attention throughout the estate and surrounding community. According to the local newspaper, "Banks of pipes of all sizes are located at various points in the villa and about the grounds and with the heavy stops playing may be heard for a distance of more than a mile."[72]

The prairie-styled Fabyan villa – having seven rooms, two enclosed porches, three baths, and a partially exposed basement with living quarters for servants – differed sharply from the European-style mansions and sprawling rural estates favored by Chicago's other millionaires. The era's typical estate, wrote architectural critic Barr Ferree, was "a sumptuous house built at large expense, often palatial in its dimension, furnished in the richest manner, and placed on an estate, perhaps large enough to admit of independent farming operations."[73] Most were based on designs from Europe's past, reflecting historical Gothic, Tudor, Georgian, and Italian Renaissance styles.

The nouveau rich of the late 1800's and early 1900's, according to one historian, "sought acceptance by the old, monied families on the East Coast by purchasing the accoutrements of cultural refinement and emphasizing family tradition."[74] Most treated their estates as hobbies and advertisements of their wealth. For instance, Ogden Armour, the meatpacking tycoon, bought 1,000 acres in Lake Forest, about ten miles north of the city, where he stocked his two lakes with perch and bass and pretended to operate a ranch, yet in reality his Melody Farm was more for

GEORGE FABYAN

show than work. (The house today is the main building for the Lake Forest Academy, an elite private school.) Colonel Robert McCormick, owner of the *Chicago Tribune*, arranged his Cantigny estate largely for horseback riding and fox hunts, although he reported regularly from there on the virtues of rural labor and living. Fabyan, in contrast, designed his villa in a modern style with an architectural radical, and the Riverbank lands were regarded as "one of the most successful experimental farms in the state."[75]

The colonel often began his days just to the east of the villa at a 110-foot-tall flagpole, where the Stars and Stripes was raised each morning at seven and then lowered precisely at sunset. The daily ceremonies featured the ritualistic folding of the flag and the firing of a small brass cannon. Fabyan even hired a musician to blast a bugle through a post-mounted megaphone for morning reveille and evening taps, yet the other workmen so despised the noise they harassed the bugler until he quit his job and moved off the estate. The patriotic colonel also placed a sign on the path near the flagpole: "Men passing here will please salute the flag."

Nearby were Egyptian-styled and hieroglyphic-emblazoned armchairs, benches, tables, and pedestals that overlooked the pit used in the summer to house the colonel's alligators, which were transported each winter – upside down and in burlap sacks – to the south greenhouse. Scattered throughout the property were the rest of Fabyan's menagerie – including show dogs, tropical birds and peacocks, Louie the Wolf, three bears (one named Mary who loved pumpernickel bread), red-suited monkeys (one of which stole watches and wallets from female guests, and another periodically pinched pretty women), as well as a baboon and its pet dog. The collection represented one of the world's odder private zoos.

The animals frequently frightened Fabyan's employees and visitors. One of the chauffeurs, for instance, picked up a female guest at Chicago's Midway Airport for the trip back to Riverbank. It being winter, the driver paid little attention to the woman's full-length coat. When Fabyan greeted her warmly at the estate, however, she removed her garment to reveal a nine-foot-long bull snake coiled around her arm.

A bit further down the path from the villa laid an intricate Japanese garden, which Fabyan began building in 1910 with the help of a gardener presented by the Japanese royal family in thanks for the colonel's kindnesses. Fabyan, in fact, long enjoyed a special relationship with Japan, having acted as that country's informal consul in the Chicago area before an official consulate was staffed. During Theodore Roosevelt's peace negotiations to end the Russo-Japanese War, the colonel served as the U.S. contact with Baron Jutaro Komura, Japan's minister of foreign affairs and head of that country's delegation at the Portsmouth, New Hampshire, conference. A few years later, Fabyan hosted at Riverbank General Kuroki, commander of Japanese forces in Manchuria and Russia, and in 1910, he did the same for Kan-in-no-Miya, a prince within Japan's royal family and a young son of Emperor Mutsuhito.

Riverbank's Japanese garden featured a Shinto Shrine, a Torii gateway at the west entrance, and a ritual water basin next to the tea house, which was made of Douglas fir. A small half-moon bridge united two goldfish ponds and represented unity; being steep and difficult to climb, it symbolically tested a visitor's religious zeal. In order to suggest snow, Fabyan added white cement to cap replicas of Mt. Fuji and Mt. Sumeru, the mythical center of the Buddhist universe. Lanterns marked the garden's several paths and lighted the visitor's passage through time, while big rocks surrounding the pond represented the resting places of mortal souls. The garden's outer pathway, with stairs and small bridges, provided numerous vistas that encouraged visitors to forget their worldly concerns, while the inner garden around the actual tea house offered a quiet sanctuary that broke one's connection to the outer world. Yet not being strictly bound by traditional Japanese design, Nelle and the independent Fabyan couldn't help adding Victorian gazing balls they found attractive.

The garden came alive in spring, with yellow-flowered Winter Aconites and white-drooping Snowdrops popping out in early March, followed over the coming weeks by cherry blossoms, the starry bright-blue flowers of the Siberian Squill, as well as multi-colored azaleas. Migratory birds – including the Scarlet Tanager, Rose-Breasted Grosbeak, and Baltimore Oriole – added song to the brilliant colors.

The Fabyan estate also included two large greenhouses, both of which profitably grew flowers that Nelle shipped daily to Chicago hotels, restaurants, and markets. Her favorite were roses, including Columbias and Killarneys, and the colonel hired Charles McCauley, a nationally recognized rose-growing expert from the U.S. Department of Agriculture in Washington, D.C., to tend to the flowers and hybridize various species, several of which won horticultural awards. (McCauley, like most Fabyan employees, displayed multiple talents, his other most noteworthy being innovative means of dynamiting Riverbank's stone quarries.)

The main garage housed, at various times, Fabyan's Rolls Royce, Bentley, Stevens Duryea, and two Cadillacs, as well as Nelle's roadster. The car barn featured a turntable that allowed several automobiles to fit into stalls. Two chauffeurs lived on the top floor, and each stressful morning, one would rush the colonel to the Geneva station, where the frequently late millionaire would sprint to catch the 7:32 am express train for the 60-minute ride downtown. Another driver and Fabyan's city limo stayed in Chicago, ready to pick up the businessman each day from the Northwestern train station and take him to Bliss Fabyan & Company. (On a few occasions when not running late, the playful colonel enjoyed being driven to the Geneva station in a cart drawn by two white mules.)

The boat house, connected by tunnel to the Fox River, protected *The Lady Nelle*, a rough-bottomed racing scull, as well as a motorized launch, an 18-foot sailboat, two Indian birch-bark canoes, several small fishing boats, and a couple of rafts used to transport supplies and cattle across the river. The first floor's ceiling could open, allowing hoists to raise the boats for winter storage. The structure also served as one of the stops for the interurban trolley.

That building and its contents were controlled by one of Riverbank's more colorful characters – Jack "The Sailor" Wilhemson. A credentialed Norwegian seaman, this tall, strong showman regaled Riverbank guests on river tours with folksongs and yarns, and at staff parties, he regularly dressed the nautical part in starched whites, danced the jib, and entertained the estate's children by tying virtually every known knot.

A bit to the north of the boat house, enclosing a path from the villa to the bridge and the Fox River island, draped a long grape arbor, about six feet high and half the length of a football field. Large lawns, composed of Kentucky blue grass, graced both side of that arbor.

The bridge itself suffered a difficult history. Tired of having to pull, poll, or paddle flat boats across the river with cattle and cargo, Fabyan requested a building permit from the U.S. Army Corps of Engineers but was denied because federal bureaucrats considered the Fox to be a navigable river, even though it ran shallow in most spots. The frustrated colonel eventually used his political connections to obtain an act of Congress allowing the bridge's construction, leading the wry-humored Fabyan to add a 30-foot-tall lighthouse on the island's north tip for the benefit of the supposed "navigators." The copper-domed structure consistently flashed two beams, then three, then two, then three, and so on – the colonel's way of saying "Twenty three skidoo" or "keep off." Fabyan ordered the lighthouse to wink continuously as long as he lived.

In January 1916, not long after the colonel completed a second concrete bridge from the island to the eastern shore, an all-night downpour launched a rush of river ice that broke the structure into several sections and carried them south. Reporting on the Fox River rampage, a local reporter declared "the damage done at the Riverbank estate of Col. George B. Fabyan is enormous."[76] The colonel quickly built a sturdier replacement, which still stands today.

Dominating the Isle of View's south side was a massive Roman-styled swimming pool, fed by the same artesian well that supplied the neighboring

GEORGE FABYAN

icehouse, causing some to complain it was almost too cold to enter. A double row of Doric columns, connected by a narrow wooden trellis, surrounded the pool and appeared to be an ancient temple, and lights atop the colonnade provided illumination for night swimming. The chauffeur's daughter, Ethylmarie Williams, taught the employees' children to swim. As was the style, women at the pool wore knitted undergarments under an outer tunic of silk, and Fabyan demanded they don long stockings.

A 12-foot pedestal just to the west of the pool featured a massive eagle sculpture, identical to the one above the acoustics laboratory. They were the works of Silvio Silvestri, Riverbank's staff artist and Nelle Fabyan's tutor.

Across the river, on the property's east side, ran tracks of the North Western Railroad, which periodically delivered boxcars full of unclaimed or damaged merchandise for the colonel's collection. In fact, Fabyan's favorite structure on his vast estate was marked by a distinct sign – TEMPLE DE JUNK. He informed a reporter that the 35-by-45-foot warehouse was the "most important thing in the place," and salesman then asked the journalist, "Want to buy some plows? Here are 75 I'll sell you."[77]

Much like a child on Christmas morning, the colonel expressed great delight whenever opening unmarked boxes of treasures. According to Don Williams, who grew up on the estate, "We used to spend hours climbing over that stuff, looking over it. It was part of his hobby to use the things that he found. Once, he got a shipment of portholes, so he made windows in the lab out of them. Once, he got vault doors so he put one on his office."[78]

In addition to the contents of random freight cars, the acquisitive Fabyan purposely sought out animals (both stuffed and alive) and Indian artifacts, yet he was not a particularly careful collector. Consider the mummy the colonel proudly displayed at both the villa and lab. One day a visiting archeologist suggested the Egyptian body was fake because its torso seemed awkwardly shaped and much larger than typical Middle Eastern specimen. Riverbank researchers promptly placed the "mummy" on a stretcher and took it for an X-ray. Some collectors might have been disappointed to learn there was no skeleton beneath the wrappings, yet the Riverbank curator boasted, "You can go to any museum and see a real mummy. Where else will you see one that's fake."[79]

The Fabyan farm provided four sources of income: beef, chickens, milk, and flowers from the greenhouses. Cattle roamed throughout the eastern fields, fenced in by gates where the railroad line crossed the colonel's property. Also throughout Riverbank's east segment were low wooden huts for the estate's 300 ducks as well as 15 chicken houses built on skids to hold 18,000 White Leghorns as well as several dozen Rhode Island Reds and Buff Orphingtons. The colonel shipped poultry and eggs daily to Chicago markets and restaurants, including the prestigious Union League Club where he was a member. Fabyan also raised and sold pigeons, and his dairy herd provided milk to the estate and surrounding towns. To satisfy his own robust appetite, to feed his employees, and to entertain his frequent guests, Fabyan also maintained an ample supply of hogs, sheep, and turkeys.

The east side's most prominent structure was a 68-foot-high, eight-sided Dutch windmill. Although in significant disrepair when the colonel purchased it for $8,000 in 1915, he spent another $75,000 (totaling almost $1.6 million in today's dollars) to move and reconstruct the structure. The colonel directed Bert Eisenhour to supervise the marking of the timbers for disassembly at the York Center site and reassembly in Riverbank, and the transporting crew deployed a team of mules and an extending wagon to bring the long uprights to the Fabyan estate. The colonel himself spent countless hours fussing over the construction, to the point he required the carpenters to find replacement floorboards that matched the original wood grains. Fabyan also insisted on hard maple floors and fir wainscoting, luxuries usually reserved for expensive homes. "Money was no object," marveled one of the craftsmen.[80]

Originally built in Lombard, Illinois, in 1876 in a traditional Dutch style, the Fabyan Windmill was a fully automated wind-driven mill with clever belt-run elevators moving grains from floor to floor and from chutes to hoppers. The structure included three working floors, a wide exterior platform that wrapped around the second floor, as well as rooms for lodging

GEORGE FABYAN

(it was where William Friedman stayed when he arrived at Riverbank to conduct genetics research). A grand coal-fired double oven could simultaneously bake 72 loaves of bread Fabyan sold to his ration-hungry neighbors in paper bags during World War I.

The building was featured in 1980 on a 15-cent postage stamp, part of a five-part series the U.S. Postal Service entitled "Windmills USA." One historian called the Fabyan structure "the best example of an authentic Dutch windmill in the United States; actually it's a treasure and would be among the most popular windmills in the Netherlands."[81]

The colonel's motivation for spending more than $1.6 million on a windmill is not clear. He told one reporter he simply wanted wholesome whole-wheat bread from freshly ground flour, "I'm going to start in feeding myself, my family, and my guests with real bread, something I've been hankering after for years. That flour is going to cost about nine times what flour retails for, but it will be worth the price."[82] Yet the colonel's milling efforts ceased along with World War I's flour rationing. It seems, says today's self-guided tour brochure prepared by Kane County, Fabyan simply "wanted to build a beautiful and romantic monument to grace the eastern shore of his estate."[83]

The colonel was happy to share the estate's grace with others. Despite the lighthouse's ominous warning, he kept his lands (other than the island and the swimming pool) open to the public, only asking visitors to stay on the paths. One Geneva resident remembered that after Sunday dinner "your day was not complete unless you took a pleasant stroll at Riverbank."[84]

Visitors to the estate enjoyed their strolls but also gained an insight into Fabyan's diverse personality. The old Dutch windmill, Paul Sabine stated, "stands as a reminder of a rich man's fancy." Yet, boasted the researcher, the Riverbank Laboratories "stand as a reminder of the same rich man's hard common sense."[85]

Chapter 5
ACOUSTICS

Sound was one of the diverse subjects that fascinated Fabyan, and he instinctively understood it was a form of energy he could measure, manipulate, and even see. Promising to perfect auditoriums, synchronize telecommunications, and "find a cure for deafness," he declared, "We've been ... pioneering all the way; carving our own path; slowly unearthing the secrets of nature."[86] Yet loud noises troubled the colonel, who feared they shortened the lives of city dwellers, and he waged battle against the "racket ogre" as "a humanitarian task."

It was with these mixed goals Fabyan initially approached Wallace Sabine to examine and fix his gravity-bound levitation machine, whose synchronized musical strings were to vibrate vigorously and reverse gravity. (More on the Sir Francis Bacon-inspired levitation chamber is in the next chapter.) The Harvard physicist briefly examined the colonel's device, tested the sound from its various strings, and quickly concluded it would never rise. Although disappointed in Bacon's design, Fabyan appreciated honest answers from bright scientists and offered to build Sabine a state-of-the-art acoustics lab in the quiet surroundings of Riverbank, "out in the prairie where there just isn't any noise." When Sabine asked questions about the

GEORGE FABYAN

facility's possible design and provisions, Fabyan responded, "Hell, what do you want? I'll build it."[87]

Fabyan first encountered Sabine when Harvard, which his family supported, asked the young physicist to correct the disruptive echoes within the new lecture hall at its Fogg Museum. Despite no academic training with sound, Sabine began measuring the room's reverberation, or the time needed for different frequencies to become inaudible. Working throughout the night when students and researchers would not make unwelcome noise, he tested the sound-absorbing qualities of chairs, curtains, wallboard, and a variety of other materials, moving them from different classrooms and then transferring them back in the early morning before teaching began again. Sabine calculated, for instance, that six seat cushions decreased reverberation time about as much as the average person's body and that "the absorbing power of the cushions when touching edges was less than when separated."[88]

The work demanded persistence and accuracy. Sabine, as an example, had to discard 3,000 observations, representing two months of work, because he failed to account for how his own clothing absorbed sound. Only later did he realize his wool coat skewed the room's results because it absorbed more sound than when he wore just a cotton shirt. Moving forward, his testing outfit included the same blue jacket and vest, wool trousers, high shoes, and thin underwear.

For three years, from midnight until 5 am every other night, Sabine played an organ pipe to fill the lecture hall with the pitch of 512 vibrations per second, equal to the note of C on a violin. He then cut off the organ, listened until he could no longer hear the reverberation, clicked his stop watch, and recorded the duration of audibility. He subsequently extended his investigation to notes ranging from three octaves above to three octaves below violin C.

Living with his mother on Garden Street in Cambridge, Sabine spent his free nights in the house reviewing data. One Saturday evening, he declared triumphantly, "Mother, it's a hyperbola." What he realized was when he multiplied the number of cushions and the room's reverberation time the results were constant, meaning he could devise a mathematical formula for reverberation that resulted in a basic hyperbolic curve. In more scientific terms, Sabine wrote: "The duration of the residual sound in a particular room was proportional inversely to the absorbing power of the bounding walls and the contained material, the law being expressed closely by the formula — $(a+x)t = k$ — the formula of a displaced rectangular hyperbola."[89]

By studying rooms with good acoustics, the physicist concluded concert halls needed reverberation times between 2 and 2.25 seconds in order to deliver "rich" music to the audience. Lecture rooms, in contrast, required slightly less than 1 second. Sabine initially found the spoken word within the Fogg Museum's troubled lecture hall remained audible for a lengthy 5.5 seconds, forcing listeners to experience a jumbled cacophony of 12-15 words from a talking professor. To correct for this echo and resonance and to reach the desired 1 second, the physicist installed enough sound-absorbing materials to cut the room's reverberation time some fivefold.

Fabyan praised the Fogg success. So did Henry Lee Higginson, the wealthy financier who owned the Boston Symphony Orchestra and wanted to build a new and more acoustically advanced auditorium since the city planned to bulldoze a road through the existing Music Hall. Higginson, attracted to both music and science, introduced Sabine to Charles McKim of the prominent architectural firm McKim, Mead and White, which had been chosen to design the new Symphony Hall. Even though Sabine criticized McKim's initial plan for a semi-circular amphitheater, the proud architect was "much impressed by the force and reasonableness of (Sabine's) arguments, as by the modest manner in which they were presented."[90]

Sabine convinced McKim and Higginson to shorten the hall, add a second gallery, and surround the main chamber with buffer corridors that would restrict exterior streetcar and traffic noise. He also suggested the stage and balcony be made shallow in order to help distribute the sound evenly to all the seats, and he specified wall niches and ceiling coffers that would scatter the sound uniformly. To maximize the audience's acoustical experience, he even advised on the kinds of seats and the placement of organ pipes.

Symphony Hall opened on October 15, 1900, with 2,000 concertgoers marking the new century's seriousness about music as well as its commitment to science. The devout music listeners had worried the structure would not live up to their high expectations for a secular temple to worship symphonic masterpieces, yet the *Boston Sunday Journal* reported: "Doubt as to the acoustic properties of the hall were dispelled. Solo instruments were heard with delightful distinctness; the bite of the strings was more decided than in the old hall, and the ensemble was effective without muddiness or echo."[91] The *New York Evening Post* praised the structure as "what very few concert halls are – a success acoustically."[92]

Not everyone, however, appreciated this monument to acoustical discipline. The *Musical Courier*, a small journal written in New York City, criticized the hall, but less for its sound than for the idea "science" should tinker with a great symphony. "Music is art and art cannot be measured beforehand," stated the paper. "If music could always sound as we before its issue could predict by formula X+N=Y, why then it would no longer be music."[93]

The Science of Sound

Fabyan scoffed at such criticisms of science. Only by collecting data and developing mathematical formulas, he argued, could men and women enjoy music, dramas, and speeches within acoustically balanced auditoriums. He expressed confidence sound could be manipulated for the betterment of audiences.

An avid collector, the colonel acquired an extensive set of books and articles on the history of acoustics. He particularly admired Pythagoras, the Greek mathematician living in the 6th century BC who first observed sound caused vibrations. Pythagoras calculated that the width of a plucked string's blurred area determined the musical instrument's loudness. The more

ACOUSTICS

motion the string produced, the more noise humans perceived, and without any vibration, the instrument stood silent. Pythagoras also noted shorter strings vibrated more rapidly and produced shriller, higher-pitched notes.

Aristotle around 350 BC added the insight that vibrating strings struck the surrounding air, which also moved the neighboring bit of air, suggesting sound needed air or some other medium in order to be transmitted. A vacuum without such a substance, the philosopher declared, would not conduct sound.

The Roman engineer Marcus Vituruvius Pollio further suggested sound caused the air to vibrate, not just to move. He argued these air vibrations were what our ears perceive as sound.

Fabyan felt sound also could be seen. Building on the work of Rudolph Koenig, who won the gold medal at London's 1862 Crystal Palace Exposition, the colonel, trying to picture sound's vibrations as flickering flames, had sound waves refract a beam of light that passed through a special box and then fell on to a photographic plate, thereby providing a snapshot of the music or speech. Still, Fabyan, as well as Sabine, ultimately felt sound was something to be heard rather than visualized, concluding the "ear itself … (gave) a surprisingly sensitive and accurate method of measurement."[94]

Numerous others, of course, advanced the science of sound. John Shore and Rudolph Koning in the early 18th century developed tuning forks that provided constant vibrations or tones, although Riverbank researchers in the early 20th century greatly improved the technology. Christian Doppler in the mid 19th century calculated how pitch changes when a sound's source moves toward or away from a stationery listener. Ernst Mach in the early 20th century calculated the speed of sound through air, and a number mentioned after his name defines how fast an object is traveling compared to that speed.

Sound moves at different rates in different mediums. It travels more quickly, for instance, along a steel rail (5,941 meters per second) than through the air (331 meters per second), and it's a bit faster when the atmosphere is warmer since the air's density decreases.

We measure a sound's intensity in decibels (dB), a scale that matches what we perceive subjectively as loudness. Since the scale is logarithmic, a sound ten times louder than the threshold of hearing has an intensity of 10 decibels, but one 100 times as loud has an intensity of 20 decibels. To be more specific, a whisper has an intensity level of 15 dB, while rock music reaches 120 dB. Eardrums rupture at 160 dB.

Pitch is measured according to the frequency of the sound wave, with high frequencies producing higher notes. Middle C has a frequency of about 261 Hertz (or cycles per second), while the slightly higher note E comes in at around 330 Hz. Human audibility ranges from approximately 20 Hz to 20,000 Hz. Dogs can hear (and often howl at) higher frequencies.

Tinkering with acoustics, of course, was not a new exercise, and Sabine and Fabyan were far from the first to demonstrate sound can be reflected or absorbed. The Roman Vitruvius wrote a ten-volume exposition on architecture, including an analysis of an amphitheatre's acoustical qualities. Using simple ratios that tried to recreate the universe's divine order on a human scale, Vitruvius encouraged his contemporaries to structure their forums and amphitheaters in order to channel sound so audiences could best hear the speakers and performers. The great Renaissance scientists also explored sound's components, with Isaac Newton calculating the conduct of vibrating strings and Galileo Galilei measuring sound's speed through the air, water, and different mediums.

Scientific investigations of the 18th century coincided with the emerging commercialization of theater, particularly in Europe where music playing had been restricted for centuries to small rooms controlled by royals. As more common folk became interested in instruments and as entrepreneurs realized they could profit by delivering performances to the masses, the demand grew for theaters that were both larger and able to deliver good acoustics. Marking the trend was the transition from Margrave's Opera

House – built in 1748 for only 450 courtly listeners – to Milan's La Scala – built just 30 years later for a mass audience of almost 2,300.

In the United States, music in the 18th and 19th centuries became embraced by the middle class yet controlled increasingly by professionals. The shift away from amateur musicians resulted from a variety of cultural and social forces, including new technology, urbanization, and a romantic movement that embraced art appreciation as ennobling.[95] The proliferation of the phonograph, for instance, allowed listeners to enjoy recordings by paid singers and professional orchestras, resulting in the slow displacement of self-made music.

Up until the mid 19th century, popular concert halls and opera houses featured dances and sermons as well as concerts, whatever was needed to sell tickets and make money, and audiences during musical performances regularly chatted and whistled along. Social reformers, such as John Sullivan Dwight, who wrote the *Journal of Music*, tried to enrich the musical experience and instill a measure of respect for great compositions. Boston, as Sabine's work at Symphony Hall demonstrated, was a center for such enrichment efforts, as evidenced by the *Evening Transcript's* declaration that the city "does not take her music frivolously, but as a service, an education."[96]

The era's Victorians also shifted the justification for music appreciation from personal enjoyment to social improvement. According to historian Emily Thompson, "Children were given music lessons in order to instill character and discipline, not to inspire creativity and joy. The young women who performed in the parlors of Victorian America similarly demonstrated virtue more than virtuosity."[97]

Theories abounded about the best acoustical design for theaters that could deliver great music and instill morality. Believing large spaces demanded amplification if ticket payers were to hear the performers, Frenchman Pierre Patte argued for an elliptical shape that would allow the walls to reflect and augment the sound. An elliptic, he reasoned, would double the impact of a speaker or singer as sound rays from the performer were reflected from the auditorium's walls.

British architect George Saunders favored an oval shape, although he arrived at his recommendation after a bit more experimentation. Asking the question, "In what form does the voice expand," he placed a speaker outdoors in an open space and then he circled that sound source while calculating the furthest distance at which he could hear clearly. Italian Count Francesco Algarotti, in contrast, felt a semicircular theater would best magnify voices from the stage.

In the era before loudspeakers, most acoustical architects worried performers would provide too little sound within large theaters, so they sought designs that would amplify voices rather than retard reverberation. In fact, Patte, Saunders, and Algarotti specifically warned against using sound-absorbing materials. Sabine and Fabyan changed that perspective.

The physicist and the colonel demonstrated different rooms demand different acoustics. Orchestra conductors want structures with a fair amount of reverberation in order to make the music lively. Dramatic actors, in contrast, prefer the least possible echo so their every word can be heard distinctly. Lecturers and motion-picture engineers also want minimal reverberation so their sentences and musical themes do not become mixed and muffled. Noting these disparate demands, Sabine wrote, "The question as to what constitutes good and what constitutes poor acoustics is not a question in physics," yet designing a room to meet its acoustical needs, he argued, does require science.

Even noted architects and scientists, however, floundered when it came to the difficult task of designing for sound. Benjamin Latrobe's Capitol Building, which opened in Washington, D.C. in 1807, suffered "a very material defect in the hall of the House of Representatives. The voice of the speakers is completely lost in echo, before it reaches the ear. Nothing distinctly can be heard from the chair or the members."[98] The next Capitol version, completed after the British burned Latrobe's structure in 1812, offered few acoustical improvements, even though designers tried numerous alternatives, including one that reversed the seating arrangement of the elected representatives. In 1853, when Secretary of War Jefferson Davis decided to expand and improve the structure in order for "the voice from each member's desk shall be made easily audible in all parts of the room," he turned for advice to Joseph Henry, then secretary of the Smithsonian Institution and the nation's chief scientist. Henry, who had previously examined the sound-absorbing properties of several materials, concluded the refurbished auditorium's acoustical "principles … are correct, and that they are judiciously applied."[99] Unfortunately, those principles offered no enhancement for the actual speakers and listeners, and many years later Sabine was called in to provide the needed improvements.

Only a few architects instinctively understood sound. Dankmar Adler, one of the best, first demonstrated his skill when helping to reconstruct Chicago after the great fire of 1871. In partnership with Louis Sullivan, he built the Auditorium Building in Chicago, Carnegie Hall in New York City, and dozens of other theaters and auditoriums. All were judged acoustical successes.

The Auditorium Building, considered "a complete expression of the needs of its own environment – the excitement and energy of late 19th century Chicago,"[100] included a 4,000-seat theater, ballroom, convention hall, hotel, and offices. To promote the passage of sound, Adler arranged ceilings and walls to direct vibrations back toward the audience, yet to avoid echoes, he avoided hard, smooth surfaces. When the auditorium opened on December 9, 1889, Adelina Patti, opera's reigning diva, declared, "The acoustics are simply perfect."[101]

Adler certainly possessed a basic understanding of the science of sound and the conservation of energy, yet his success resulted largely from intuition. According to Sullivan, "It was not a matter of mathematics, nor a matter of science. There is a feeling, perception, instinct, and that Mr. Adler had. Mr. Adler had a grasp of the subject of acoustics which he could not have gained from study, for it was not in books. He must have gotten it by feeling."[102]

Sabine instead relied upon experimentation. He began by clarifying the goal of the building's owners and performers and then carefully tested how a room's design and materials could best obtain that objective. Consider his efforts at the Sanders Theatre. Sabine asked several pianists and conductors to evaluate the room's acoustics as he adjusted the number of sound-absorbing cushions. All agreed 13 cushions made the piano seem lifeless. Sabine took away two cushions and everyone heard "a perceptible change for the better in the piano music." Three more removals and the effect continued to improve. Four more were taken away, leaving only four cushions, but the reverberation then was too great. So Sabine brought back two cushions, making a total of six, and the musicians agreed the sound was "the most nearly satisfactory."[103]

Not trusting instincts, the physicist offered mathematics. Having calculated the hyperbolic parameter "k" to be proportional to the room's volume, he devised a formula ($k=0.164V$) that allowed architects to adjust the space's size and materials until they achieved the desired acoustical result.

Sabine also devised the basic measurement of absorption. Since a square meter of an open window reflected no sound back into the room, it represented the perfectly absorbent material and was given the absorption measurement of 1.0. Sabine then calculated the coefficient to be 0.061 for pine sheathing; 0.034 for plaster; and 0.025 for brick. Stated differently, bricks absorb 2.5 percent of the sound energy hitting them and reflect 97.5 percent back into the room. "When one considers that a difference of 5 percent in reverberation is a matter of approval or disapproval on the part of musicians of critical taste," stated Sabine, "the importance of considering these facts is obvious."[104]

An auditorium's most significant sound absorber, of course, is its audience. A man in ordinary clothing, Sabine and Fabyan discovered, absorbs slightly less than a woman, while people wearing heavy coats suck up more. Larger audiences tend to improve an auditorium's acoustics since they reduce reverberation, yet they also diminish the sound's loudness or intensity.

If sound is not absorbed, it is reflected and sent back across a room until it meets another surface or sound wave. As Sabine wrote, "At any one time and at any one point in the room there are many sounds crossing each other." Not unlike water waves in a pool, the sounds can be neutralized if the crest of one and the trough of another meet. The complement of such an interference phenomenon is when two sound waves are added together and amplified; in technical terms, "when two sounds of the same pitch are superposed in exact agreement of phrase, the intensity of the sound is the square of the sum of the square roots of their separate intensities." These merging sound waves can cause some regions within an auditorium to be comparatively loud or quiet, and they explain a room's so-called hot and deaf spaces.[105]

Sound can be partially managed by the theater's structure, its furnishings, materials placed on walls and ceilings, and the audience's arrangement. According to Sabine, "The size and shape of the theater determines the distance travelled by the sound between reflections, while the materials determine the loss at each reflection."[106] The combination of reverberation, interference, and resonance certainly complicates a room's acoustics, yet, stated Sabine, "it is a rational engineering problem" solved by adjusting "the shape of the auditorium, its dimensions, and the materials of which it is composed."[107]

Other factors are at play, too. Consider the British House of Parliament, which had placed heaters in between the rows of speakers facing each other, so when an orator's words struck this rising column of warm air part of the sound was transported upwards and "reached the auditor diminished in intensity." Sabine's rather simple solution was "distributed floor outlets" for heating and cooling.

The industry producing acoustical building materials grew steadily in the early 20th century, largely because Sabine, Fabyan, and several others experimented with fabrics and objects that could restrict reverberation and improve sound quality. One early and widely advertised product – called

GEORGE FABYAN

Cabot's Quilt and marketed as "the first thing ever scientifically made for deadening sound" – featured a thick layer of grass lodged between two sheets of heavy building paper. The quilt, described as impervious to decay, vermin, and fire, was placed within a building's walls and between floors in order to prevent sound from penetrating among rooms.[108] Sabine devised his own hair felt for the Fogg Lecture Hall, and a slew of other companies experimented with jute, cotton, and wool, and they marketed an array of products with names such as Florian Sound-Deadening Felt, Kelly's Linofelt, and Keystone Hair Insulator, described as "thoroughly cleansed" cattle hair sandwiched between layers of fireproof asbestos sheathing.[109]

Working with Raphael Guastavino, Sabine in February 1913 patented the Rumford tile, distinguishable for its "peculiar porosity, characterized by interconnecting air spaces." The physicist calculated the new material absorbed 29 percent of incident sound, far more than the 3 percent captured by Guastavino's traditional tiles. He first applied Rumford tiles at St. Thomas Church on Fifth Avenue in New York City, where parishioners long had complained about being unable to understand sermons reverberating off the large vaulted spaces lined with hard, reflective surfaces. Perhaps as important for style-sensitive designers, the new tiles displayed the same look, feel, and texture of conventional masonry, allowing Sabine to describe Rumford tiles as "a new factor at the disposal of the architect."[110]

Wallace Sabine

Wallace Clement Sabine and George Fabyan certainly weren't the only contemporary scientists investigating the properties of sound. Indiana University's Arthur Foley, University of Illinois' George Stewart, and Lehigh University's William Franklin were part of a growing group of acoustical researchers that attracted increased interest at the start of the 20th century. In fact, the president of the American Association for the Advancement of Science (AAAS) admitted in his 1901 annual address that "this branch of science has been comparatively neglected by physicists for many years," and he declared it his "duty to direct some attention thereto."[111]

Sabine, nonetheless, may have been sound's most meticulous and practical researcher. Rather than speak at academic conferences or write for scientific journals, he targeted the architects and contractors who needed to understand acoustical design options. He appreciated they had numerous concerns other than a structure's sound quality, yet his articles in building-trade publications encouraged them to consider acoustics early in their design process.

This applied physicist devised for designers and builders the generally accepted equation for reverberation time – the room's volume (in cubic feet) times 0.049, divided by the product of the room's surface area and the average absorption coefficient of its surfaces, equals the number of seconds needed to drop the sound's intensity by 60 decibels. That formula is still used to gauge a room's acoustical quality, and appreciative scientists named the international unit of sound absorption "the sabin."

The Harvard and Riverbank physicist moved acoustical design from an exercise based on guesswork to one reliant upon science. According to the Franklin Institute's *Journal,* his success "came as a result of the skillful and persistent application of the scientific method to a problem that had not before been the object of any thoroughgoing scientific attack."

Sabine's building credits included the chamber for the U.S. House of Representatives, West Point's chapel, the New England Conservatory of Music, and Rhode Island's State Capitol. He helped architect Stanford White block the persistent echo within John Jacob Astor's indoor tennis court. At the request of William Mead, he also soundproofed a room for Joseph Pulitzer, who, according to the architect, "is a nervous wreck and most susceptible to noises, and he has discovered many real and imaginary noises in his house. Some of them are real and can be obviated, and we have great confidence that you (Sabine) can discover the cause and a remedy for them."[112]

Sabine also advised numerous corporations, such as the Remington Typewriter Company that wanted to quiet its machine's clatter. However, some companies that wanted to influence Sabine's results and control the messaging, such as United States Gypsum, backed away when the hard-nosed scientist declared "the only condition on which I would undertake the work was that the results, whether favorable or unfavorable to them, should be published."[113]

Sabine climbed the academic ladder quickly. Born in 1868 in Richwood, Ohio, he displayed intelligence early and benefitted from a mother who exhibited an "abnormal conscientiousness in the exercise of her maternal duties."[114] He studied physics and graduated from Ohio State University at the age of 18, moved (with his mother, who had abandoned her less-ambitious husband) to Harvard for graduate school, became an assistant, then an instructor, and within a decade the Hollis Professor of Mathematics and Natural Philosophy. Sabine initially explored the characteristics of electricity and instinctively connected aspects of this form of energy to light, heat, and sound. He lectured at the Sorbonne, obtained an honorary doctorate from Brown University, became a member of the National Academy of Sciences, vice president of the American Association for the Advancement of Science, and vice president of the American Physical Society. Academic colleagues described Sabine as "a meticulous experimenter guided by the highest ideals of scientific integrity," and they hailed him as "a gracious and dedicated man, at once reserved and intense."[115]

Colonel Fabyan promised this distinguished scientist a sophisticated laboratory, well away from the maddening sounds of Boston's streets. Sabine accepted the offer and set strict specifications for his quiet chamber, yet before enjoying his Riverbank lab the acoustical specialist signed on as a World War I advisor to the U.S. Navy in order to help minimize the sound of U.S. submarines and airplanes. As a staff member within the Bureau of Research for the American Expeditionary Forces, he also developed cameras that captured aerial reconnaissance of German trenches and airfields. For these diverse efforts, Sabine received the French Legion of Merit Medal and earned the rank of colonel within each of the four Allies.

World War I accelerated acoustical research. In order for soldiers to obtain early warning of a German airplane's faint drone, Sabine and his colleagues devised large arrays of listening horns, and they equipped sailors on patrol boats with equipment to differentiate the sound of a U-Boat's propeller from that of other ships or schools of fish.

Sabine loved the work, but the war years proved hard on him. From a physical perspective, he was diagnosed with a kidney disorder, but he refused surgery, declaring he did not have time "while my country is in danger."[116] The stress of combat also imposed a lasting mental toll on this driven but mild-mannered scientist. One afternoon after he returned to Cambridge, an agitated Sabine took his files into a Harvard courtyard and burned them in a small bonfire. According to a colleague, "The severity of the criticism which Professor Sabine always applied to his own productions increased with time, and it is to this extreme self-criticism and repression that we must ascribe the loss of much invaluable scientific material."[117]

Sabine settled into Riverbank just before Christmas of 1918 and immediately began calibrating Fabyan's new test chamber, which was the world's first laboratory devoted exclusively to research in acoustics. The era's unsophisticated testing equipment required a researcher to sit within a wooden crate that looked something like a steam box and ensured his body and clothing did not affect the acoustical measurements. Day after day, Sabine or a colleague would sit in that box with a stopwatch, calculating the time between the striking of an organ note and when that sound could no longer be heard. His only other tools were a pencil and pad to record the data. According to John Kopec, an acoustical engineer who later worked at Fabyan's estate, "In the Riverbank test chamber, the low frequency of 100 hertz (Hz) (the sound of a transformer hum or a fog horn) takes almost 7 seconds [for the sound to decay 60 decibels], and the high frequency of 5000 Hz (the sound of a whistling tea pot or a navy boatswain's pipe) takes approximately 3 seconds."[118]

Sabine, commended by a colleague for his "unending patience and untiring energy,"[119] never finished the Riverbank calibrations – which required 1,100 calculations for each of the organ's 73 notes. In January 1919, when visiting Harvard, Wallace Sabine succumbed to kidney cancer. He was 50 years old.

The colonel, with a brand new acoustics laboratory and no one to run it, turned again to Harvard for help. Having access to university officials because of his family's significant contributions, Fabyan located Paul Sabine, a distant cousin of Wallace who had specialized in spectroscopy. Paul was thrilled to carry on his relative's work, and he wrote to a friend, "It appears that this Colonel Fabyan is very wealthy, patriotic, and quite involved in various scientific endeavors."[120] Paul arrived in Geneva in February 1919, at the age of 40, and began completing the 80,300 calculations needed to calibrate the sophisticated laboratory. This meticulous scientist, in fact, tested the room several times to demonstrate repeatability and to ensure the chamber's qualities had not changed. "This may seem excessive," Paul Sabine wrote without sensing the understatement, "but when one considers the number of variable factors, and the extremely fundamental character of this work for all measurements that are to follow, extreme care justifies itself."

Paul Sabine

Paul Sabine was born in January 1879 in Albion, Illinois. He graduated from Harvard, taught for six years at the Worcester Academy, returned to Harvard for his Ph.D. and to become an assistant instructor, and then took a position at Case School of Applied Science in Cleveland, Ohio. During World War I, he helped the Navy calibrate wind tunnels in order to design airfoils for the NC-3 and NC-4 flying boats that made some of the first successful transatlantic flights.

Sabine arrived at Riverbank praising his more famous cousin, writing a lengthy and gushing tribute in *The American Architect:* "To have accomplished so much in the span of a relatively short life demonstrates the great mental force of the man and the sheer grit and indomitable will."[121] In

1936, Paul even admitted to some level of "hero worship," but stated, "I can only plead that Wallace Sabine was one of those rare natures who inspired that attitude in all who knew him."[122]

The colonel and the scientist argued regularly about the lab's tactics and plans, yet Fabyan seemed to give Sabine a relatively free hand as long as it appeared he was advancing the science of acoustics. Paul, meanwhile, often praised his benefactor, as in the dedication to his *Acoustics and Architecture* where his "friend Colonel George Fabyan" was thanked for his "generous support and unfailing interest in the solution of acoustical problems."[123]

Sabine prepared monthly reports for Fabyan, often highlighting his challenges and needs. Shortly after his arrival, he complained about how difficult it was to train researchers to take precise sound observations, particularly "in this Sound Chamber where the rate of decay is small, making the instant when the decaying sound crosses the line of minimum audibility hard to determine with precision." The organ note, in fact, remained audible for only about four seconds, and the average deviation from the mean was just 0.11 seconds. As a result, only Paul Sabine and Bert Eisenhour conducted most of the time-consuming measurements.

To steer clear of variables, Sabine ensured the box and organ remained the room's only fixtures. Temperature variances also were avoided, and Sabine and Fabyan spent substantial effort and expense keeping the chamber between 58 and 68 degrees, a notable feat considering Chicago's bitterly cold winters and hot muggy summers, as well as the era's lack of sophisticated (and quiet) room heaters and air conditioners.

Once the room was satisfactorily tested and calibrated, Sabine began measuring the impact of adding various items, such as hair felt, fibers, balsam wood, and plasters. "When a sound wave enters an absorptive material, such as a mineral fiber," he wrote, "the pressure from the wave causes the fibers to vibrate, accomplishing work. In doing work, heat is dissipated and the energy of the sound wave is exhausted. The energy transfer is from sound-pressure wave energy to mechanical vibrating energy to thermal energy."[124]

GEORGE FABYAN

Sabine and Fabyan initially tested a hodgepodge of materials, including layers of lasagna, laundry lint, and oatmeal. Yet Riverbank quickly attracted corporate clients – such as Owens Corning Fiberglass and the National Door Manufacturer's Association – willing to pay for reliable acoustical tests they could use to promote their products as effective sound absorbers.

The colonel also thought his acoustical lab would be a training and research center, like a university, and he identified Sabine as "dean." Yet as profit-making testing opportunities developed, Fabyan changed his mind and listed Paul as "laboratory director."

Whatever the title, the colonel wanted Riverbank Laboratories to be renown, so, building on his Washington contacts, he convinced the National Research Council to form a Committee on Acoustics that met in 1922 at Fabyan's estate. In addition to enjoying the colonel's fine cuisine and wine, the panel of leading sound scientists identified 13 topics for further study, ranging from aiding navigation to transmitting music.

Fabyan and Sabine also encouraged their manufacturing clients to adopt testing standards with common metrics, and they helped form the Acoustical Materials Association, whose charter members included Johns Manville (the maker of asbestos and sound-absorbing wallboard), American Piano Company, and American Telephone & Telegraph. That group, after a fair amount of competitive squabbles among company representatives, agreed to a controlled sequence of tests that would be reviewed by an independent technical committee, to which Sabine was elected chairman.

The Riverbank team also tried to organize scientists and engineers into the Acoustical Society of America (ASA) in order to encourage communication and cooperation among the growing number of acoustical researchers, including those at Bell Telephone Laboratories, National Bureau of Standards, Berlin's Heinrich Hertz Institute, and England's National Physical Laboratory. The ASA first met in December 1928 at Bell Laboratories in New York City and initially attracted a bit more than 450 members, but that number increased to almost 800 by 1932. The association included "a mingling of many disciplines besides acoustical engineers and acoustical physicists; there were psychologists; there were musicians, otologists, phoneticians, and you name almost anything associated with acoustics, and there was representation there."[125]

Fabyan and his team also devised several instruments to measure sound. For instance, they modified the Toeppler-Boys-Foley method of photographing air disturbances, Eisenhour created a photometer to gauge sound mechanically, and F.W. Kranz invented a means to calibrate the human ear. Speaking to a reporter, the colonel boasted, "Dr. Kranz here has made a machine – it was a year's work – that measures the sensitiveness of the human ear without the chance of human error under which the ear specialist is handicapped."[126]

While work progressed at Riverbank, American Telephone & Telegraph and the radio divisions of General Electric and Westinghouse developed new technologies to ensure telephones and radios provided clear signals. Their condenser transmitter, for instance, measured and quantified sounds, and their electric transducer transformed acoustical energy into electrical signals as well as converted those signals back into sound.

Such new equipment quickly transformed acoustical research as evidenced by comparing Wallace Sabine's laboratory – with only a pipe organ and his own ears – to Paul Sabine's – complete with "linear response microphones, vacuum tube amplifiers and oscillators, sensitive alternating current meters, and telephonic loud speakers." Much of the transformation resulted from the electrification of sound, a development Alexander Graham Bell advanced in 1876 with the telephone's introduction, placing sound in an electric wire and allowing two people to communicate across vast distances almost instantaneously. Amplification followed quickly, as evidenced by the addition of horns and loudspeakers to Guglielmo Marconi's radio, thereby allowing communal listening.

Even auditoriums and music halls were altered by what one historian described as the "powerful combination of architectural and electrical control over sound."[127] When massive loudspeakers delivered an orchestra's music to a 12,000-person crowd at Lewisohn Stadium in New York, some feared the new equipment would provide only "unlimited volume," yet the audience welcomed the "full tones with a radio sound similar to a movie theatre vitaphone."[128]

Radio City Music Hall, which opened within New York's Rockefeller Center in December 1932, perhaps best symbolized the architect's growing control over sound. The huge arches shaping the proscenium contained thousands of tons of Kalite Sound Absorbing Plaster that blocked reverberation, yet they also hid modern loudspeakers that delivered clear and distinct sound to the 6,200 listeners. The massive air conditioners and other mechanical equipment were isolated structurally in order to eliminate unwanted noise. Reviewers, as a result, raved that everyone in the audience could hear "quite well, even from the seats furthest from the stage."[129]

Acoustical engineers actually manipulated Radio City's sound, enhancing, for example, the orchestra's string section or adding a bit more crowd-pleasing base. The music critic for the *New York Times* marveled that "fifty 'ribbon' microphones are on the stage, each with an amplifier beneath the stage that can be regulated at will." Ironically, the sound heard on opening night was not the direct voices of the singers or the orchestra's notes, but, like what an audience member would hear on her home phonograph, the voices and notes were reproductions rendered by amplifiers and loudspeakers.

The Edison Company, in fact, sponsored Tone Tests to demonstrate the quality of such acoustical re-creations. At concert halls across the country, including Carnegie Hall in New York City, engineers broadcast music from an Edison Diamond Disc Phonograph and then the assembled orchestra would play the same piece. While audiences marveled, the clever Edison marketers declared their electrically manipulated sound had evolved beyond "canned music" and was equivalent to – or even better than – a live performance.

Movies

Fabyan, encouraged by his celebrity guests, also experimented with sound for the emerging motion picture industry. Thrilled with the new technology, he encouraged his Riverbank researchers to help provide more profound ways to tell stories and transmit information to audiences.

Hard to imagine today, but early acoustical experts argued vigorously about how best to record the voices of actors. On one side of the debate, Paul Sabine suggested engineers seek "acoustic conditions for recording which will produce a record that most nearly simulates music and speech as heard by an audience from an actual stage."[130] He asserted, for instance, that a discussion in a living room should sound distinct from one on a busy street, and Warner Brothers's first "all-talking" movie, *The Lights of New York,* released in 1928, provided this mix of sounds as the scenes moved from a dance hall to a barber shop to Central Park. Other acoustical engineers argued against a "natural" representation that varied voices and noise depending upon the shot, preferring instead a uniform sound that could be obtained from boom-suspended microphones that tracked close-up scenes or from concentrators for far-away shots.

Sabine and Fabyan designed an early "talkie" studio in New York City as well as the first sound stage in Hollywood. Paul also served as a consultant to the Fox-Case Corporation and presented a paper in 1926 to the Society of Motion Picture Engineers explaining the acoustics of recording rooms. Although the Riverbank team couldn't eliminate echoes entirely, they lined early soundstages with thick blankets and sound-absorbing tiles in order to limit reverberation times to below 0.50 seconds.

A new breed of motion picture engineers, however, relied more on electro-acoustics than on architectural materials to control sound on movie sets. Placing less emphasis on noise-absorbing tiles and curtains, they managed their recordings through the placement of microphones and the regulation of loudspeakers. They also developed ways to mix and filter sound electronically, and they devised methods to fade and dissolve voices and music as the action moved from one scene to another. By the 1930's, according to historian Donald Crafton, a movie's sound track "came to be seen more as an ensemble constructed in postproduction rather than as a record of an acoustical performance."[131]

Technological advances certainly altered the science of sound. Modern vacuum tubes, oscillators, and amplifiers replaced organs and tuning forks, and relay-controlled acoustical clocks displaced stop watches, allowing engineers to avoid sitting for hours in an enclosed box trying to listen with their own ears to a fading sound. Yet the Riverbank team achieved remarkable precision with unsophisticated equipment, causing one modern acoustician to argue, "The only real gain over the years has been the amount of time needed to conduct the tests, an economic rather than scientific advance."[132] Even the engineer who challenged Sabine's formulas for ultra-low reverberation rates stated, "The general conclusions reached in the pioneer work of Prof. Wallace Sabine have not been materially altered."[133]

Radios, Auditoriums, and Building Materials

In addition to improving movies, George Fabyan and Paul Sabine helped radio stations perfect their broadcasts. In 1926, for instance, they arranged for Chicago's WLS station to transmit the same program but with reverberations varying from 0.25 to 0.64 seconds. Sabine predicted "the tendency toward less deadening and longer reverberation times has grown up," and the results proved him out, as most listeners preferred the 0.64-second broadcast.

Riverbank's team, as well as other sound engineers, also redesigned movie theaters to account for the growing shift from silent films to talkies. Most film houses had been "mere barren halls with plaster walls and ceilings, wood or concrete floors, and bare wood seats," essentially with nothing to restrict the reverberation of sound from the newly-installed loudspeakers. The Electric Research Products Incorporated (ERPI), a division of Western Electric, calculated a movie theater's reverberation time needed to be much shorter than that for a music hall offering live performances, yet a good bit longer than Sabine's radio broadcast. ERPI recommended 1.25 seconds for a theater seating some 1,200 viewers and 1.75 seconds for the largest rooms with 6,000-person capacities. To reach those levels, theater chains invested thousands of dollars to upholster seats, hang drapes and tapestries, and install sound-absorbing plasters and tiles on walls and ceilings. Because many small-scale operators could not afford those expenses, independent movie houses declined.

The design of music auditoriums also changed throughout the 1920's in response to the new electro-acoustical equipment as well as the audience's growing preference for the sounds they heard from their radios and phonographs. The new halls – including the Chicago Civic Opera Auditorium, Rochester's Eastman Theatre, and Cleveland's Severance Hall – featured a small stage that spread out increasingly toward the audience. This fan shape acted like a horn, and acoustical consultants concentrated their sound-absorbing materials toward the back of the auditoriums in order "to surround the audience in a reverberation-muffling blanket." Their goal was to "blend and unify the music at its source and then transmit this music efficiently and uniformly throughout the extended seating area."[134]

Riverbank Laboratories continued to test and accredit sound-absorbing materials, yet Fabyan faced increased competition, including from the government-supported National Bureau of Standards, which in 1922 established an acoustical division in order to set industry-wide principles. Meanwhile, physicists at the University of California, Los Angeles (UCLA), proposed their own methods for testing the sound-absorbing qualities of building supplies, and the American Standards Association tried to find agreement among acoustical engineers on appropriate testing instruments.

The building materials industry also became increasingly competitive with an ever expanding number of sound-absorbing tiles, masonry, plasters, and rigid wallboards – with such descriptive, if convoluted, names as Corkoustic, Audicoustone, Silen-Stone, Moucoustic Plaster, and Acoustifibrobloc. Paul Sabine, in fact, developed "Sabinite," a sound-capturing plaster the U.S. Gypsum Company began marketing in 1926.

Architects enjoyed the options provided by these building-material competitors. Howe & Lescaze in 1932, for example, integrated many sound-absorbing features into the Philadelphia Saving Fund Society (PFSF) Building, in part to muffle the noise from the first air conditioning system within an office tower. Electrical chilling had been developed by Willis Carrier and others in the early 20th century, yet initial applications tended to be limited to humidity control at industrial sites, although movie theaters in the 1920's increasingly offered their patrons "manufactured weather." Reviewers celebrated the PSFS Building as a thoroughly modern structure, "inside and out," because its complex technological systems controlled the temperature, air flow, light, as well as sound.

Howe & Lescaze also incorporated acoustical tiles into the PFSF Building's ceilings in order to block reverberation, and they "hermetically sealed" walls to obstruct street sounds. Ironically, such measures made the PSFS Building so quiet engineers decided to wire each office for radio reception and to install scores of small speakers. According to historian Emily Thompson, "The silence of architectural acoustics combined with the sound of electroacoustics to complete the modern soundscape."[135]

Noise Control

Fabyan and his Riverbank colleagues sought to extend to everyday life the silence made possible by architectural acoustics. Sabine felt the "inevitable noise" from "the ever increasing congestion of living and working conditions of modern life" would lead to "the constant wear and tear upon nervous and mental power."[136] Paul declared "sound control" to be of "vital importance" and worthy of "the time and labor necessary to secure the quantitative data required for its solution." He saw acoustical research as having a social aim, "directed toward the alleviation of the evil of noise and the enhancement of the enjoyment of speech and music."[137]

Unwanted noise had increased substantially since Riverbank Laboratories began testing acoustical materials. The Roaring 20's literally roared with radio loudspeakers, automobile horns, train and factory whistles, as well as low-flying airplanes broadcasting persistent advertisements. Doctors warned the constant urban din endangered mental health, and efficiency experts calculated a substantial loss of productivity.

"There is nothing fanciful in the assertion that the pitch of modern life is raised by the rhythmic noise that constantly beats on us," protested the *Saturday Review of Literature* in 1925. "No one strolls in city streets, there is no repose in automobiles or subways, nor relaxation anywhere within the range of a throbbing that is swifter than nature," declared the magazine. The lament was part of a larger complaint about urban life – "Our nervous hearts react from noise to more noise, speeding the car, hastening the rattling train, crowding in cities that rise higher and higher into an air that, far above the grosser accidents of sound, pulse with pure rhythm."[138]

The power of new instruments to measure sound more accurately increased the desire of engineers to control urban noise. They calculated subways could squeal at 120 decibels, considered to be the threshold for pain, while trucks idling along city streets emitted more than 80 decibels. "Noise reform," in fact, became part of the progressive agenda that tried to curtail urban sprawl, cut pollution, and improve public health. In an era that worshipped efficiency, sound engineers also sought to eliminate excessive noise in order to enhance prosperity. New York City officials approved a variety of ordinances limiting the cries of newsboys, the honking of automobiles, and the racket of loud radios, and they substituted silent traffic lights for whistle-blowing police and installed quieter subway turnstiles at many underground stations. Yet the health department, unable to clearly define when sound was excessive, issued no fines in response to more than 5,000 annual noise complaints.

A few citizens actually found the increasing noise to be a sign of progress, something to be embraced as modern. Asserted one writer in the *New York Times Magazine*, "Civilization, the greatest of all achievements, is by that token, of all, the most audible. It is, in fact, the Big Noise."[139]

Unable to control the modern racket, many architects turned inward and tried to control sound within private spaces, making apartments and commercial buildings acoustical refuges for city residents. Yet the modern office increasingly resonated with typewriter clacks and telephone bells, and the effect, complained one executive, was "an unbearable increase in unnecessary noise, confusion, and nervous excitement, which has had a marked effect on the normal efficiency of both executives and office workers."[140] Sound-control businesses saw an opportunity. Johns-Manville, for instance, claimed its Acoustical Correction had a remarkable effect: "It produces a sense of comfort and quiet and of relaxed nerve tension which is hard to describe in words." The company advertised its quieting treatment paid for itself in increased productivity within just a few months.

Fabyan and Sabine turned even more inward in their crusade to assist the hearing impaired. While trying to block the din for most urban residents, the tycoon and the scientist understood thousands needed help to hear any sound or to recognize speech, music, and other joys of life. Part of Sabine's motivation resulted from his own difficulty noticing certain high frequencies, such as a telephone ring, but mostly because his wife, Cornelia, needed ear surgery in order to improve her hearing. His first article on the subject, "The Efficiency of Some Artificial Aids to Hear," appeared in November 1921,[141] and he and Fabyan spent a good part of the 1920's developing hearing trumpets, and Sabine later helped create the electronic hearing aid.

Tuning Forks

When not helping the deaf, making movies, tackling urban noise, or testing sound-absorbing materials, Riverbank researchers developed the world's finest tuning forks. Their devices, in addition to harmonizing pianos and other musical instruments, still are used to test human hearing, maintain time in those computer clocks with quartz crystals, provide vibration treatments to patients, calibrate police radar guns, as well as synchronize the transmission of electricity.

Technically known as acoustic resonators, most tuning forks appear to be U-shaped bars with two prongs attached to a handle, all usually made of steel or an alloy. When struck, each fork vibrates and resonates at a constant pitch, determined by the length and thickness of the prongs. Perhaps the most common fork emits a frequency of 440 Hertz (Hz), or 440 cycles per second, otherwise known as the note A from the violin's second string, the viola's first string, and an octave above the cello's first string. Concert masters use this common or concert pitch to coordinate orchestras.

As the prongs vibrate, they bend slightly but rapidly. When they turn outwards, they compress the surrounding air, increasing its pressure, and when they bend back inwards they offer more space for the air and cause lower pressures to form. When tracked by scientists, these movements from a tuning fork's vibrations produce a perfect sine wave formation.

The handle vibrates only slightly, allowing the fork to be held without the sound being dampened. The equipment, however, often sits atop a resonator, usually an hallow rectangular box that amplifies the sound. Without a resonator, each prong's sound waves, which are out of phase, tend to cancel each other out. In fact, the volume actually increases when a sound-absorbing sheet is inserted between the prongs and reduces this cancellation.

John Shore is credited with inventing the tuning fork in 1711. No ordinary British musician, he served as Sergeant Trumpeter to the royal court, and his musical skills were so admired that George Frideric Handel and Henry Purcell wrote orchestral pieces specifically for him.

More than 200 years passed before Shore's invention was substantially improved. Up until the early 20th century, German firms were considered to be the premier makers, but their steel forks slowly rusted, leading to shifts in frequency. Some engineers had tried to enhance the steel forks with nickel or chromium plating, yet the resulting equipment often peeled and altered the fork's pitch.

Largely because of Fabyan's whim to test whether foreign-cast bells were of superior quality to those produced in U.S. foundries did Bert Eisenhour, Paul Sabine, and other Riverbank researchers develop more reliable tuning forks. Their early efforts focused on the use of aluminum alloys that offered lighter weight and freedom from rust, and in 1932 Eisenhour patented a bimetallic, temperature-compensated tuning fork. Although Fabyan by then suffered from lung cancer and was less involved in Riverbank's research, he encouraged Eisenhour and Sabine to report on their discovery in a May 1936 paper to the Acoustical Society of America entitled "Control of Temperature Variation in the Frequency of Tuning Forks."

The Riverbank innovation, which achieved previously unobtainable accuracy, sparked an array of developments. The Associated Press, for instance, could now synchronize its transmitters and receivers and fax photographs. Early facsimile machines produced distorted transmissions because temperature differences caused the steel tuning forks to fluctuate. Those early machines, in fact, required the forks to be housed within temperature-controlled "ovens," yet wire-service photographers often were unable to maintain constant temperatures in the field and, therefore, could not transmit pictures of breaking events.

More reliable than conventional equipment, the new turning forks also enabled radio and television stations to drive their show tapings at constant speed. Moreover, they permitted the development of more precise time pieces (such as the Bulova Company's Accutron watch) as well as more accurate measurements for the speed of cars and airplanes. Also notable, they led to ultra-precise frequency controls vital to missiles, satellites, and other equipment for the American military, advancements that pleased the patriotic colonel, who also helped the armed forces make and break codes and ciphers.

Chapter 6
CIPHERS, SHAKESPEARE, AND LEVITATION

In addition to sound, Fabyan long had been interested in secrets – keeping his and stealing others. As a young boy, he crafted various codes to hide information from his proper parents and pesky brother. When he reentered the family business, he quickly devised elaborate means to ensure his company's finances and transactions were protected from competitors, and he began purchasing a substantial library on cryptography, including rare texts from the 16th century. That interest, as will be explained in the next chapter, foreshadowed the colonel's groundbreaking achievements in military ciphers, yet it also left him open to questionable theories about how his hero Sir Francis Bacon concocted elaborate codes to hide history-shattering assertions, such as the scientist being the illegitimate son of Queen Elizabeth or the real author of plays attributed to William Shakespeare. The mercurial colonel ended up spending more than 11 million in modern dollars to prove Bacon hid such messages within the books he published.

Fabyan was not the only early-20th-century tycoon expressing interest in Sir Francis Bacon's ciphers. Walter Conrad Arensberg, who bequeathed a substantial collection of modern paintings to the Philadelphia Museum of Art, wrote *The Cryptography of Shakespeare* and argued: "The conclusive evidence that William Shakespeare is the pseudonym of Francis Bacon is incorporate in the original editions of the Shakespeare plays and poems. This evidence consists of cryptograms in which the name of the poet is signed as Francis Bacon." Kate Prescott, another Boston Brahmin close to the Fabyan family, also spent years trying to highlight Bacon's genius. She was described as "a kind of contact woman in the Baconian underworld, or, to vary the metaphor, the liaison agent between the American cells of international anti-Stratfordianism."[142]

Yet not only rich eccentrics questioned Shakespeare's authorship. The search for the true writer became "the Greatest of Literary Problems" debated by such distinguished writers as Walt Whitman, Henry James, Mark Twain, and Sigmund Freud. At least 15 prospects were considered the actual author, with much attention throughout this long-lasting craze devoted to Edward de Vere, the 17th Earl of Oxford; and William Stanley, the 6th Earl of Derby. Still, within the more than 4,000 separate books and articles by anti-Stratfordians the favored candidate, largely because of his genius and varied interests, has been Francis Bacon.[143]

Sir Francis Bacon

Fabyan's inspiration for Riverbank Laboratories resulted, in large part, from Bacon's blueprint for a multi-disciplinary research center. The colonel even engraved the English philosopher's famous mantra – "Knowledge is Power" – above his sound lab's entrance. He also adopted Bacon's dictate that science should transcend the quest for personal power or riches in order to aid the general public; the "true ends of knowledge," wrote Bacon, are to "seek it not either for pleasure of the mind, or for contention, or for superiority to others, or for profit, or fame, or power, or any of these inferior things; but for the benefit and use of life; and that they perfect and govern it in charity."[144]

Noting Sir Francis' essays and books on arts and sciences, as well as his roles as a canny politician, legal scholar, and high-minded statesman, biographers typically pronounced him to be a "universal genius." Thomas Jefferson ranked Bacon, along with John Locke and Isaac Newton, as "the three greatest men that have ever lived, without any exception, and as having laid the foundation of those superstructures which have been raised in the Physical and Moral sciences."[145] Charles Darwin claimed his *The Origin of the Species* was based on "Baconian principles."

Those principles form the foundation for the modern scientific method, a disciplined approach to inquiry. Bacon, in fact, sought to enlarge knowledge by devising the now-common tactic of collecting data and then developing axioms and insights.

While best known for broad essays on the wonders of science, Bacon also completed his own pragmatic experiments. For instance, he devised ways to weigh air and water, to separate and compound metals, and to "conserve oranges, lemons, citrons, pomegranates etc all summer."

Sir Francis battled against religious zeal, superstition, and tradition, especially his era's virtual worship of Aristotle and classical learning. Compared to the Greek philosopher's embrace of deduction, or arriving at conclusions through reasoning, Bacon preferred induction, whereby he developed principles only after making observations and testing facts. He criticized Aristotle's syllogism as mere mind games, preferring instead the direct investigation of nature. Rather than "hunt more after words than matter," Bacon advanced the "slow and faithful toil (that) gathers information from things and brings it into understanding."[146]

The Englishman sought nothing less than to restructure traditional scholarship and to shift scholars from studying books to examining nature. He claimed this approach – involving the persistent collection of data – would shine "a light that would eventually disclose and bring into sight all that is most hidden and secret in the universe." One biographer found that Bacon, "more fully than any man of his time, entertained the idea of the universe as a problem to be solved, examined, meditated upon, rather than as an eternally fixed stage upon which man walked."[147]

In his quest to reform learning, Bacon sought to elevate the prestige of science, or what was then known as natural philosophy. He divided human knowledge into three key categories: History, Poesy, and Philosophy, which he associated with three "faculties" of the mind: memory, imagination, and reason. Discounted history as the mere accumulation of facts and poesy (or literature and art) as only "feigned history," Bacon argued genuine advancement of learning would occur only if the prestige of philosophy (and particularly natural philosophy) was elevated while history and literature (in a word, humanism) were reduced.

Another distinction between Aristotle and Bacon was the Englishman's belief empiricism and induction would produce practical knowledge for "the use and benefit of men" as well as the relief of human suffering. The Greek philosopher, at least according to Bacon, was content with purposeless debate and lacked a master principle behind his philosophy.

In one of Sir Francis' early essays, *The Proficience and Advancement of Learning*, he criticized his contemporary intellectuals as stagnate and irresponsible. He suggested his new methods of thinking would open their minds and eyes to the world around them, providing insights and achievements that would improve the human condition.

Unlike his contemporaries, Bacon was an optimist. As one biographer put it, "Most English and European intellectuals were either reverencing the literary and philosophical achievements of the past or deploring the numerous signs of modern degradation and decline."[148] The poet John Donne, for instance, lamented, "Our age is iron, and rusty too." Bacon, seeking to escape such darkness and decay, declared a brave new dawn of scientific advancement.

In addition to science, Bacon felt law could enhance society, and he sought to create a great renewal of legal principles. In his roles as parliamentarian, solicitor general, attorney general, and chancellor, he consistently tried to make the law more understandable and reasonable, and he worked to codify rules and decisions, to link law and logic, and to analyze leading cases in order to highlight their underlying principles.

Francis was born in London in January 1561 to well-connected parents. His father, Sir Nicholas, sat on the Privy Council and was Lord Keeper of the Great Seal under Queen Elizabeth, who was a neighbor and family friend. His mother, Ann Cooke, served as governess to Prince Edward and was sister-in-law to Lord Burghley, Elizabeth's Chief Counselor and perhaps England's most powerful man. Ann also wrote verses, read French, Italian, Latin, and Greek, and managed to dominate her five sons.

Both Francis and his older brother Anthony suffered weak constitutions. Anthony was lame and almost lost his vision at age 14, while Francis spent extended periods in bed. Yet both, especially Francis, were recognized early for their intellects. While quite young, Francis wrote to his uncle Lord Burghley that "all knowledge" was his province, and he entered Cambridge's Trinity College at the youthful age of 12. Francis already possessed set opinions, and he mocked his tutors as "men of sharp wits, shut up in their cells of a few authors, chiefly Aristotle, their Dictator." Even Queen Elizabeth noted Bacon's precociousness and referred to him as "the young Lord Keeper."[149]

At the age of 15, Francis convinced his father's friend – the new British ambassador to France – to appoint the young college graduate as an embassy attaché. In addition to his academic and diplomatic responsibilities, Francis used the independence from family and school to dabble extensively, with one of his creations being a cipher that translated all the alphabet into combinations of "a" and "b." This "biliteral" system used only these two letters, yet Bacon represented each of the alphabet's 26 characters with groupings of five "a's" and "b's." Within Francis's secret writings, the letter "A" became "aaaaa," while "Z" was "babbb."

Although Bacon did not publish anything about this ingenious cipher until 1623, he spent countless hours perfecting his ability to hide messages. In its simplest form, a note reading "Hi" would be presented as "aabbb abaaa." Yet anyone intercepting such a substitution cipher could, with enough patience and text, translate the message. So, according to historian William Sherman, Bacon's "way around this problem was as powerful as it was simple: he allowed the "a's" and "b's" to designate the different forms of anything that can be divided into two classes, sorts, or types (which Bacon referred to as the 'a-form' and the 'b-form.')"[150] Those different forms could be pluses and minuses, dogs and cats, carnations and roses, or, as Fabyan would later demonstrate, human bodies facing different directions on the steps of the Aurora Hotel. According to Bacon, the biliteral system provided the power "to represent anything by means of anything. ... and by this Art a way is opened, whereby a man may express and signify the intentions of his mind, at any distance of place, by objects which may be presented to the eye, and accommodated to the ear."[151]

Bacon provided the following example that employed two different fonts, or what he called a "bi-formed alphabet," with the cover text cleverly saying the opposite of the intended warning for a secret agent to flee. The 15-letter text — "**Do** n**o**t **go** til I c**o**m**e**" – becomes "aabab ababa babba" when "a's" are bold letters and "b's" are in regular font. That three-letter text, when translated, becomes the intended message: "Fly."

When Francis was 18 (in 1579), his father, Sir Nicholas Bacon, died unexpectedly after catching a chill from sitting by an open window during a February freeze. Sir Nicholas had set aside substantial funds to purchase an estate for Francis, as he had done for his four older sons, yet he passed away before signing the necessary papers. Francis, as a result, received just one-fifth of his expected inheritance and quickly got himself into debt and was forced to return home from France.

As one biographer noted, young Bacon was "without fortune, without physical attractiveness, and without profession." To make a bit of money, he began in 1579 to study and teach law at Gray's Inn, a professional association for barristers and judges. Two years later, he won election from Cornwall to the House of Commons, where he remained a member for 37 years.

Despite Queen Elizabeth's early accolade, she never warmed to Francis, in part because the young politician spoke out in Parliament against excessive subsidies to the royals and their favorites. Bacon, nonetheless, persisted in trying to ingratiate himself by writing numerous thoughtful essays and "letters of advice" on domestic and international issues. He also pushed his friends and relatives to lobby the queen for appointments, yet she gave the attorney generalship and solicitorship to others.

Bacon subsequently turned for political and economic help to Robert Devereux, the Earl of Essex and a one-time favorite of Queen Elizabeth. The earl needed an advisor and was willing to serve as Francis' financial patron. Unfortunately for Francis, Essex suffered a few problems, not the least of which was the failure of his troops to subdue the Irish. Much more damaging, however, was his quite public assertion that the English throne was being sold to the sons and daughters of the Spanish king. Worried that an angry queen and her supporters were trying to kill him, he raised a small army of 300 men, a fact that further displeased Elizabeth, who had him captured, imprisoned, and executed.

Here's where Bacon demonstrated his cold and calculating political skills. Recognizing Elizabeth did not want a public backlash against her actions, Bacon agreed to write the legal exposition justifying the execution. Yet also realizing Elizabeth would not much longer be monarch and her likely successor would be James of Scotland, who liked Essex, the shrewd Bacon also wrote an *Apologie* defending his role in the Essex trial.

Bacon's prospects, in fact, soared when James became king in 1603. He was knighted that same year, appointed Solicitor General in 1607 and Attorney General in 1613, became a member of the Privy Council in 1616, selected Lord Keeper of the Great Seal (the same post held by his father under Elizabeth) the following year, and in 1618 reached the ultimate political position of Lord Chancellor. Adding titles to his resume, he also was named Baron of Verulam (in 1618) and Viscount of St. Albans (in 1621).

King James and Sir Francis shared many similarities and developed an immediate rapport. According to historian Wigfall Green, "James, having become the king of Scotland when only one year old, had been, like Bacon, nurtured in the gentle manner and tutored by the most learned scholars of his nation. Both men were, in physical appearance, less than attractive; both were ceremonious; both were – to use a word from James' vocabulary – 'pawky,' or sly or humorous. Both spoke and wrote well."[152]

GEORGE FABYAN

Yet Bacon, usually politically astute, periodically angered the king, such as when he criticized the monopolies held by the Duke of Buckingham, who happened to be James' favorite. Moreover, Sir Francis's hard-nosed and sometimes arrogant actions as Lord Chancellor nurtured enemies within Parliament, and in 1621, his opponents coalesced and had him impeached. The 23 charges of corruption focused largely on his taking bribes while a judge, which was a rather common practice of that era. The court ordered Bacon to pay 40,000 pounds, although King James remitted the fine. Sir Francis also was committed to the Tower of London, yet his imprisonment lasted only four days, and while allowed to maintain his titles, he lost all his political offices and his seat in Parliament.

The public disgrace, ironically, increased Bacon's stature as he directed his new-found free time to scientific and literary writings. The remaining five years of his life, in fact, were his most prolific and influential. In *Novum Organum*, Sir Francis argued that his new "instrument" of scientific thinking would guide scholars beyond tradition in order to discover nature's secrets. (Portraying this notion, his book's front piece featured a ship sailing through the mythical towers of Hercules and into the unknown.) *The New Atlantis*, his science-fiction novel published a year after his death, described an ideal land of "generosity and enlightenment, dignity and splendor, piety and public spirit." Bacon's story began with sailors leaving Peru in search of a better life. Stiff winds blew them northwesterly, and they became lost in the "greatest wilderness of waters in the world" and happened to land on an uncharted island known as Bensalem, where they were welcomed by intelligent creatures who spoke Spanish, Latin, Hebrew, and Greek. The island's governor claimed the community's objective was "the knowledge of causes, and secret motions of things, and the enlarging of the bounds of human empire, to the effecting of all things possible."

The plot is thin and the writing often windy, but Bacon described an ideal science center, a vision that inspired George Fabyan. Bensalem's residents – and Riverbank's researchers – sought to advance human discovery by collecting data, conducting experiments, and applying their knowledge to produce "things of use and practice for man's life." Reflecting Bacon's evangelical ways, the island's investigators – and Fabyan's colleagues – shared their arts and inventions with others throughout the world.

Sir Francis, as noted above, displayed a strong interest in ciphers and codes, and he described their attributes near the end of his career within *De Augmentis Scientiarum*: "The virtues required in (ciphers) are three: that they be easy and not laborious to write; that they be safe; … and, lastly, that they be, if possible, such as not to raise suspicion."[153] Bacon's book, in fact, suggested how careful Elizabethan printers could place hidden biliteral messages within texts without giving any hint of deception.

Yet most printers of that period used relatively unsophisticated equipment – in which typefaces often were broken and different pages absorbed ink at different rates – that led to smudges and smears. Determining whether a particular letter was in the a-form or b-form, as a result, required a great deal of individual judgment. Since classifying the great majority of letters was uncertain, the number of alternative decipherments was large.

Still, the philosopher's cipher expertise led anti-Stratfordians, including George Fabyan, to conclude Bacon had the capacity to hide secret messages within the printed folios associated with Shakespeare and other Renaissance writers.

Some Shakespearean skeptics found an array of so-called evidence to elevate Bacon's literary accomplishments. Some said Sir Francis' letter to William Strachey outlined the structure and plot of Shakespeare's *The Tempest*. Others claimed the bard's plays offered allusions to Bacon's associates. Still others highlighted Bacon's fascination with civil history and found parallels between his unpublished writings and Shakespeare's works.

Orville Ward Owen

Fabyan was first drawn to the Bacon-as-Shakespeare theory by Orville Ward Owen, a Detroit physician who published in the mid-1890's a six-volume *Sir Francis Bacon's Cipher Story*. Noting Sir Francis's oversight of

GEORGE FABYAN

English printers, Owen focused on the odd use of italic, roman, and "swash italic" letters within various editions of Shakespeare's First Folio. The different fonts appeared to be arbitrarily placed, but Owen felt instinctively they disguised hidden ciphers.

Sensing the "cipher story" might be more widespread than just the printings of Shakespeare's work, Owen began extracting words, lines, and passages from various Elizabethan texts. He invented a machine, which he called the "wheel," to sort and arrange the coded sentences. Wound around two large spools were 1,000 feet of canvas, on which were glued 1,000 pages of selected texts arranged in ways to deliver a message that, not coincidentally, "proved" Owen's theory about Francis Bacon authoring Shakespeare's plays and sonnets.

Skeptics suggested, "The charitable can only maintain that Owen was a visionary; the less charitable will conclude that he was a mountebank. There is something to be said for the charitable; or at any rate we must maintain that if Owen was a fraud, he was a remarkably determined and consistent one."[154]

Fabyan, despite such expressions of doubt, supported Owen and financed his second expedition to Chepstow Castle, where the researcher believed the Duke of Beaufort had buried Bacon's original manuscripts. After digging through 12 feet of river mud, the venture unearthed only the foundations of a Roman bridge, yet the colonel and the doctor pressed on with other pursuits that tapped into Fabyan's joint interests in sounds and ciphers. Owen, in fact, claimed a correct interpretation of Bacon's coded writings proved Jesus Christ walked upon the water by means of high-frequency vibrations. Despite its usual praise for all things attributed to Sir Francis, even *American Baconiana* magazine dismissed Owen's gravity-defying idea: "He offered it to the U.S. Government, but it was not considered, possibly because it was classed with perpetual motion devices of ill repute."[155]

CIPHERS, SHAKESPEARE, AND LEVITATION

Mrs. Gallup

As Owen became harder to take seriously, Fabyan turned to Elizabeth Wells Gallup, a prim and proper high school principal who claimed her "scientific" techniques proved Sir Francis Bacon included informative codes within his writings and printings. Gallup persuaded the colonel to build a servant-maintained cottage at the Riverbank estate for her and her sister, Kate Wells, to hire a staff of young female assistants, and to assemble a substantial and expensive collection of Shakespearean works and documents. She even convinced Fabyan to spend tens of thousands of dollars searching throughout England for Shakespearian-era manuscripts.

Born in northern New York, Gallup studied at the State Normal College in Michigan, the Sorbonne, and the University of Marburg. She taught literature in Michigan for about 20 years before arriving, at age 65, at Riverbank. She resembled, according to a co-worker, "Whistler's Mother," and colleagues always addressed the opinionated yet formal researcher as "Mrs. Gallup." She was seen as "a woman of the old school,"[156] and another colleague described her as "a lovely person. A real aristocrat, personally. She was sincere, absolutely sincere. She really believed in what she was doing."[157]

Gallup focused on Sir Francis Bacon's membership in England's Rosicrucian Society, a group of scholars who, in that era when witches and heretics were burned, conducted their scientific experiments in secret. As overseer of the Queen's royal printing, Bacon, at least according to Gallup, devised a biliteral cipher to covertly share information among fellow Rosicrucians about recent research findings. Using two different-sized alphabets, he placed encoded text within pamphlets and publications, which only members of the Society could interpret.

Mrs. Gallup believed she, too, could interpret Bacon's codes and in 1899 published her first work, *The Biliteral Cypher of Sir Francis Bacon Discovered in his Works and Deciphered by Mrs. Elizabeth Wells Gallup*. The less-than-catchy and self-serving title attracted little scholarly attention, although it did please the ardent subset who believed William Shakespeare did not write the works attributed to him. While such theories had been floated for many years, Gallup added the veneer of science in examining Bacon's ciphers.

At Riverbank, she prepared (and Fabyan copyrighted) a 15-page brochure, entitled *Hints to the Decipherer of the Greatest Work of Sir Francis Bacon*, that offered practical guidelines for students trying to interpret the biliteral cipher. "The first requisite," wrote Gallup, "is good eyes; the second, a careful and observant attitude of mind; the third, much devoted patience." She added that "a good reading-glass, preferably oblong in shape, is a highly useful, indeed an almost indispensable mechanical adjunct."[158]

The colonel's "educational department" also published *Ciphers for the Little Folks: A Method of Teaching the Greatest Work of Sir Francis Bacon*, a 73-page hardcover book that offered a series of progressively harder lessons "designed to stimulate interest in reading, writing and number work, by cultivating the use of an observant eye."[159] Another Fabyan pamphlet for young readers was *Jerry and The Bacon Puppy*, in which a white plaster puppy, with a biliteral or Baconian cipher inscribed on its base, helps Jerry solve a secret message and prevent a crime. Fabyan used the canine sculpture, similar in form to RCA's mascot named Nipper, as a trademark on many Riverbank publications as well as in advertisements for his correspondence courses on literary cryptology and Baconian ciphers.[160]

Yet Gallup's major Bacon-is-Shakespeare report appeared in 1916 and included her translations and analyses of the ciphers within Sir Francis's short stories, poems, nursery rhymes, and scientific treatises. Fabyan published *The Fundamental Principles of the Baconian Ciphers* and dedicated it to his mother. That book attracted substantial newspaper coverage, yet several reviewers attacked Gallup's claims or questioned her sanity. Even the Bacon Council of Britain doubted her scholarship, stating, "That in view of the failure to produce satisfactory key-alphabets for the cipher narratives … and the inconclusive nature of her demonstrations, the Society is unable to give any support or countenance to the alleged discovery." Trying to deflect such criticism, Gallup wrote, "I did not find myself a Baconian until the discovery of the Bacon Ciphers answered the questions in such a final way that controversy should end. ... In giving to the world the results of my researches, I have felt ... that my work should be left without any attempt to influence or mould opinion in any other way."

The colonel, in contrast, desperately wanted to mould public opinion, and the salesman within him concluded Gallup's theories simply needed to be better publicized. He would be her agent.

As part of his public relations campaign, Fabyan invited prominent scholars to Riverbank in order to talk with Mrs. Gallup and appreciate her scholarship, or at least to keep an open mind to her claims. The colonel paid their travel expenses and treated them to fine food and alcohol.

Fabyan the salesman also placed magazine advertisements to market his so-called Riverbank School of Instruction in Deciphering. One ad headline in *Century Magazine* declared: "Use a cipher and thwart the curious." Offering either a correspondence course or personal instruction at the Riverbank estate, the announcements stated, "Twentieth century scholars found that this cipher (woven into the works of Sir Francis Bacon and other writers who lived in the time of Queen Elizabeth) opened up an entire literature to the world. And just think! You can have the fun of studying this ingenious cipher."

A far more clever (and deceitful) publicity effort featured a concocted lawsuit to restrain Fabyan from publishing materials "tending to prove" that Bacon was the real Shakespeare. The legal action was filed in 1916 by William Selig, a famous Hollywood film producer who was about to release *Romeo and Juliet*, the first in a series of planned movies based on the famous plays in order to commemorate the 300th anniversary of Shakespeare's death. Selig argued the colonel's work detracted from the fame of William Shakespeare and imperiled the success of his motion picture.

Fabyan tried to play the innocent, stating to a reporter: "I am honestly apprehensive as to where the zeal of the ardent adherents of both Bacon and Shakespeare will lead, and the effect of it on Riverbank, the home of my wife and myself, and the members of our so-called family, who are working earnestly and hard at their different tasks to add their mite to the fund of knowledge for the public good."[161] Yet the colonel used the lawsuit as an excuse to print and distribute widely a brochure, appearing to be a legal brief, promoting his view of the Bacon-Shakespeare connection.

A Chicago-based judge, Richard Tuthill, read both arguments and on April 21, 1916, sided with Fabyan, making front-page news in New York and London. "This cipher convinces me that Bacon not only wrote the works attributed to Shakespeare," the judge ruled, "but also (Edmund) Spenser's best output, (Robert) Burton's 'Anatomy of Melancholy,' and all of (Robert) Greene and (George) Peele."

It took only a short time before enterprising reporters discovered Tuthill, Fabyan, and Selig were "great cronies."[162] They also found Tuthill, as a chancery court judge, had no business reviewing a civil suit, and he had a flamboyant habit of seeking publicity. Shakespeare scholars also scoffed at the ruling; Professor Gail Kern Paster of George Washington University and the Folger Shakespeare Library laughed and commented, "Bacon must have been a very busy man."

Selig's assistant, Jack Wheeler, furthered the notion that the lawsuit was a "put up job" when a *Chicago Tribune* reporter asked about the $5,000 the movie director was ordered to pay. "Isn't that sad?" deadpanned Wheeler. "That will be about 9 million columns of publicity, won't it?"[163] Judge Tuthill eventually was censored (and his decision reversed) by his judicial colleagues, and the *Chicago Tribune* referred to the Fabyan effort as perhaps "the greatest publicity 'stunt' ever attempted."[164]

The emotional strain from the controversy – as well as the eye strain from examining minute typographic differences within Elizabethan texts – forced Mrs. Gallup to lay low and rest, yet she lost none of her self confidence and drive. On a trip to England in search of more manuscripts and evidence, she petitioned the British government to open the graves of

CIPHERS, SHAKESPEARE, AND LEVITATION

William Shakespeare at Stratford-on-Avon, Francis Bacon at St. Albans, Edmund Spenser in Westminster Abbey, and Robert Burton at Oxford's Christ Church – and she expressed genuine surprise when officials refused.

After spending four months examining the 1623 edition of Bacon's *De Augmentis*, which discusses the scientist's use of ciphers, Gallup devised a new theory – that Sir Francis placed hidden messages within the printed Shakespearean plays in order to declare he was Queen Elizabeth's illegitimate son. Since neither Elizabeth nor her successor, James I, would have welcomed such news being made public during their lifetimes, Bacon, at least according to Gallup, inserted his coded story in ways that would give historians a clue to his real heritage.

Bacon's hidden messages, wrote Gallup, are "largely devoted to a concise account of the circumstances of Bacon's birth, the mental condition of the Queen, his mother, and of the immediate removal of Bacon to York House in the care of Lady Anne Bacon. Owing to the birth shortly thereafter of a still-born child to Lady Anne, and the adoption of Francis in the place of her own lifeless infant, he became known thereafter as her own son."

Gallup didn't limit herself to Bacon's own writings and Shakespeare's First Folios. She asserted 61 different books written between 1579 and 1671 – including the works of "Ben Jonson, Rawley, and also Rawley's executor" – possess biliteral ciphers questioning Shakespeare's authorship or advancing Bacon's royal birth.

Independent researchers, and even Riverbank's other analysts, grew increasingly skeptical of Gallup's expanding claims. According to one, Gallup "often stated that things were very obvious when commenting on her findings, when, in truth, no one else could see the relationship."[165] According to Elizebeth Friedman, "Nobody's eyes ever saw what Mrs. Gallup saw."[166]

When scholars and others visited Riverbank to learn of Gallup's cryptography, Fabyan's staff, according to one, "had it borne in upon them that they should watch their tongues – with good reason, for they were becoming disillusioned with the whole affair." Another young assistant wrote: "After months of struggling without success to see her interpretation of the fonts, and to produce hidden messages of my own, my admiration for (Gallup's) facility turned to uneasy questioning, and then to agonizing doubt, and then to downright disbelief."[167]

The rather egotistical Gallup responded to such skeptics by claiming her cryptographic skills were quite rare. "Deciphering the Biliteral Cipher as it appears in Bacon's works," she boasted, "will be impossible to those who are not possessed of an eye-sight of the keenest and most perfect accuracy of vision in distinguishing minute differences in form, lines, angles, and curves in the printed letters. Other things absolutely essential are unlimited time and patience, and aptitude, love for overcoming puzzling difficulties, and, I sometimes think, inspiration."

Fabyan increasingly shifted his own attention slightly from Bacon to the Rosicrucians. According to Cora Jensen, a secretary at the Riverbank lab, "He became convinced the writings of that period were the work of the Rosicrucian Society. ... The society controlled all the printing of that period. The colonel believed that everything printed under their auspices had an underlying meaning known only to those who could decipher the code."[168] Reflecting the evolution of his thinking, Fabyan in 1929 wrote, "The so-called Baconians are interested because they expect to use the results to prove that Bacon wrote Shakespeare, and in my opinion he didn't do anything of the kind, at least not in the accepted sense of 'write' today."[169]

Gallup maintained her theories but produced no new translations. Failing eyesight and health restricted her research, yet Mrs. Gallup stayed at Riverbank until the late 1920's. The Fabyans continued to provide her with a pension until she died in 1934 at the age of 87.

Levitation

Fabyan didn't limit himself to Sir Francis's literary or hereditary claims. With guidance from both Owen and Gallup, he also came to believe Bacon-the-scientist designed an anti-gravity machine that synchronized musical strings inside and outside a cylinder in such a way vibrations created a force field powerful enough to reverse gravity and lift the shell. The colonel hired Bert Eisenhour, a civil engineer from a Chicago-based firm that built large electricity transmission projects, to construct this "acoustic levitation device" that consisted of two five-foot-long cylinders, one within the other, that rotated on a central steel rod, with musical strings mounted vertically on the outer walls. These strings were to vibrate sympathetically and create acoustic energy.[170]

Bacon's levitator, according to an acoustical expert, was based on the following principles: "If (1) musical strings are incorporated in the proper sequence on a vertically mounted cylinder, (2) the cylinder is rotated inside a peripheral outer shell assembly that contains similarly mounted musical strings, (3) the cylinder is rotated at a high rate of speed, its strings struck and set into vibration, and (4) the strings are in perfect tune with the strings mounted on the shell, then, through sympathetic vibration, the strings on the shell will also vibrate, creating a combined force field within the cavity between the cylinder and the outer shell that results in a lift force strong enough for the outer shell to levitate."[171]

Levitation tends to be mocked as unrealistic, but it does have practical and research applications. Defined as "the process by which an object is suspended by a physical force against gravity," levitation using large magnets allows special trains to rise above the rails, reducing friction and producing a smoother, faster, and quieter ride. Helicopters and hovercraft levitate by powerful downthrusts, while air hockey tables use an upthrust to float the puck. In addition to these magnetic and aerodynamic forces, sound – more accurately, acoustic radiation pressure from intense sound waves – can cause objects to suspend. Japan's Otsuka Lab has levitated objects with sound not audible to the human ear, but acoustic levitation is mostly used for container-less packaging of very-high-purity microchips and for chemical reactions too rigorous to occur in a container. Acoustical levitation theoretically could lift large objects, but current technology is limited to a few kilograms.

GEORGE FABYAN

Fabyan's rather bulky antigravity device, not surprisingly, produced sound but no upward movement; in fact, it now sits quite firmly on the floor of the Geneva History Center. According to Eisenhour, the problem lay in the spinning cylinder causing the strings to lose their appropriate tuning, so he argued the wires should be pre-tuned to compensate for the cylinder's rotation. The colonel and Mrs. Gallup, however, felt they needed guidance from an acoustical expert. As noted in the last chapter, they turned to Wallace Sabine of Harvard University's Physics Department, who quickly concluded the acoustical levitation machine would never work because the outer shell was far too heavy relative to the small amount of acoustical energy produced by the vibrating strings.

According to one of Fabyan's colleagues, "Sir Francis Bacon's stock as a scientist accordingly had a serious drop at Riverbank." The colonel turned increasingly to Wallace and Paul Sabine for acoustical research. "Colonel Fabyan," stated a Riverbank investigator, "decided there was more to be gained from promoting the work of a living scientist than in pursuing the vagaries of a dead one."[172]

That emerging pragmatism extended to Fabyan's work with codes and ciphers. Building on his patriotism and shying away from the Baconians, the colonel increasingly focused his cryptology attentions on efforts to help the U.S. military protect its secrets and capture its enemy's.

Chapter 7
SPIES AND WARFARE

Fabyan's was a life-long obsession with secret writings. "Even in his boyhood the colonel was very interested in ciphers," commented Adele Cumming, who long served as Riverbank's manager and the colonel's assistant. "They became a ruling hobby with him, and he spent a tremendous amount of money collecting old cipher books. In his collection are several originals of code deciphering books from the fourteenth century."[173] (Fabyan donated more than 1,000 such books and manuscripts to the Library of Congress, including Johann Trihemius' rare *Polygraphic* from 1518.) As a businessman, moreover, the colonel frequently used codes and ciphers to transmit sensitive information.

An earlier chapter recounted the Riverbank efforts of Elizabeth Wells Gallup, who claimed to find ciphers within the writings of Sir Frances Bacon. This chapter, in contrast, discusses Fabyan's cryptographic advances for the U.S. military and intelligence communities. That story begins with Elizabeth Friedman.

A recent English literature graduate of Hillsdale College, Elizabeth (Smith) in 1914 was working part-time at Chicago's Newberry Library when the institution received a notice that a Geneva man was looking for

GEORGE FABYAN

someone full-time to study Shakespeare's writings. She made an inquiry, and Fabyan agreed to come over. According to Elizebeth, she encountered "a large man, bearded, which was very unusual in those days, not too well dressed, but with a dashing, imperious manner."[174]

Fabyan evaluated Elizebeth quickly and virtually ordered her into his chauffeured car, which proceeded to Chicago's Northwestern train station for the ride to Geneva and Riverbank. During the train trip, the colonel thundered, "Well, what do you know?" Elizebeth hesitated, "looked at him quizzically out of my half turned head and said, in a firm by low tone, 'that remains, Sir, for you to find out.'" The answer, she noted, "pleased him and he burst forth with a loud guffaw which could be heard all over the car."[175]

Elizebeth became part of a 15-woman team that tried to discover different font types in texts from the time when Elizabeth I ruled England, with the goal of helping Mrs. Gallup prove Sir Francis Bacon wrote Shakespeare's plays. For these efforts, the young English major received $50 a month plus room and board at the Riverbank estate.

Several months later, the colonel began looking for someone to conduct genetic experiments in Riverbank's new greenhouse and adjoining laboratory. He sent notices to several college deans seeking a "would-be-er" rather than an "as-is-er," and a Cornell professor suggested William Friedman. After exchanging several letters with the colonel, the dark-haired young researcher in June 1915 moved into an apartment within Fabyan's Dutch windmill and began testing Mendel's theories and propagating diverse strains of wheat. Yet it quickly became apparent to Fabyan that William also was a talented photographer who could be pressed into service to enlarge the type in Shakespeare's folios. William, moreover, proved to be a talented code breaker, plus he seemed to enjoy spending time in the lodge with Mrs. Gallup's new assistant. As Elizebeth later wrote, "This work threw us together a very great deal, and we were married within the year."[176]

Friedman, according to a fellow code-breaker, presented a "dapper figure with the Adolphe Menjou mustache, the characteristic bow tie, and

112

the two-tone black-and-white shoes."[177] Elizabeth remembered first seeing him climbing the steps at the Riverbank Lodge and later wrote: "He was a kind of Beau Brummel, no country informality but impeccably dressed as though he had been going to a well-to-do city home."[178] William was equally meticulous in his work habits, always punctual and ever thorough, even to the point of making carbon copies of his handwritten notes.[179]

William was born Wolfe Friedman in 1881 in the small Moldavian town of Kishinev. His father, Frederic, had moved from Bucharest to become a translator – who spoke eight languages – for the Czar's Postal Service. His mother, Rosa, was the daughter of a wealthy Kishinev wine merchant. Most of the town's professionals also were Jews, who after the 1881 assassination of Alexander II increasingly worried about the government's growing religious persecutions. When Wolfe was just one year old, his father left his family and sailed for the United States, where he obtained a job in Pittsburgh selling Singer sewing machines door-to-door. Rosa, Wolfe, and his sister joined Frederic two years later, traveling steerage and escaping just before the pogroms killed scores of Kishinev Jews and destroyed 700 Jewish homes.

Frederic became an American citizen in 1896 and quickly "Americanized" his son's name to William. Although the future code breaker had no personal memory of the religious persecutions in Russia, the horror of the pogroms appeared periodically in his later writings, as did the insecurity associated with his family's constant struggle to survive financially.

The Friedmans eventually included four boys and one daughter. The mother provided most of the discipline until a domineering grandfather arrived from Russian to demand the family return to a strictly kosher diet and observe orthodox traditions. The siblings tried their best to evade or endure such restrictions.

William quite early displayed both intelligence and drive, and he claimed his fascination with codes began when reading Edgar Allan Poe's "The Gold Bug," a detective thriller.[180] Friedman graduated in 1909 from

GEORGE FABYAN

Pittsburgh Central High School with interests in agriculture and the emerging field of electrical engineering. Attracted to the Jewish "back-to-the-soil" movement, he admitted to having "notions of scratching a living out of the soil." Yet a few weeks of such scratching "showed me that Mother Nature got the wrong number when I answered the call."[181]

Since Friedman could not afford the lengthy training associated with electrical engineering, he entered the Michigan Agricultural College (now Michigan State University) and two years later transferred to Cornell University, where he concentrated on genetics, convinced he could make his mark by doubling the yield of corn crops. He stayed at Cornell for a few years to teach undergraduates and conduct graduate work on Mendel's theories of plant breeding.

It was at Cornell that Friedman first learned of George Fabyan, who, out of the blue, had written to Professor Rollins Emerson seeking recommendations for a talented researcher who could manage Riverbank's new Department of Genetics. Friedman, feeling it "advisable to start in to see how hard making a living really is," accepted Fabyan's offer of a hundred dollars per month as well as room and board at the estate. The colonel, however, refused to offer an employment contract, stating quite bluntly: "I might not like you and you might not like the job, and there is no use making a fool contract, any more than there is in signing a lease for a house, which is usually a waste of time provided either side wants to break it."[182]

Friedman appreciated Fabyan's outspokenness and even the colonel's demands that he continue his studies, affiliate with a university, and obtain an advanced degree. His early Riverbank projects focused on hatching and classifying fruit flies, as well as trying to confirm the colonel's notion that grains grow larger when planted during a full moon. In response to Nelle Friedman's requests, the young geneticist also attempted to enhance the color and durability of her garden's violets.

Fabyan, however, increasingly diverted Friedman from genetics, in large part to help fulfill the colonel's quest to prove Sir Francis Bacon was the real author of Shakespearian plays and poems. As noted before, photographer Friedman enlarged the individual letters in Shakespeare's texts, hoping a better view of the mix of italicized and regular letters would help decipher Bacon's secrets.

On his switch from genetics to cryptography, Friedman later commented, partly in jest, "I was seduced from an honorable profession to one with a slight odor."[183] No doubt the young researcher enjoyed the diversion, in large part because of Elizabeth Smith's presence in Mrs. Gallup's workshop, yet he also relished the work, writing to a friend, "When it came to cryptology, something in me found an outlet."[184] In fact, he discovered his intuitive grasp of codes and ciphers, prompting historian William Sherman to later comment, "Friedman's instant ability to work – and play – with the biliteral cipher makes his early encounter with Bacon look like Alice's encounter with the looking glass."[185]

Elizabeth, with an "e," was so named because her mother wanted to avoid the detested nickname "Eliza." She and William sparked an almost immediate attraction despite hailing from vastly different backgrounds. Descended from Anglo-Saxon and Gentile stock, Elizabeth's ancestors traveled to America in 1682 with William Penn. The family soon moved to Virginia, where peace-advocating Quakers exiled her grandfather for fighting in the War of 1812. The Smiths kept moving, with her father born in Ohio and she, the youngest of nine children, in Huntington, Indiana, then merely an Indian trading post. She studied English literature, demonstrated a quick wit and intelligence, and found a job at Chicago's Newberry Reference Library, where George Fabyan delivered his unexpected job offer.

Photographs of Elizabeth during her early Riverbank days reveal an attractive, smiling, and perky young woman. Yet William's family found nothing positive about the woman since she sparked one of the first mixed marriages within Pittsburgh's Jewish quarter. According to Friedman's brother, "You would have thought that Bill had committed murder. If he had still been living in Pittsburgh, he would have been ostracized."[186]

GEORGE FABYAN

Secrets

Although both convey secrets, codes differ from ciphers. In a code, the word "bomb" can be written as the number "66498" or the word "velvet," and the message can be translated by someone with the appropriate codebook. Ciphers, in contrast, are composed of single letters or sets of letters that symbolize the text. Put another way, a cipher is a system of communication that uses letters (or individual bits) instead of phrases, sentences, or whole words.

Both codes and ciphers have been around since men and women didn't want others to read their correspondence. Ancient Greek warriors hid their messages by writing along parchment that was wrapped tightly around a tapered staff since the unwound spiral revealed only jumbled, unintelligible letter fragments. Julius Caesar composed his secrets by substituting letters three units along the alphabet; using modern English, for example, he would have spelled "dog" as "grj."

Other men and women, of course, went to great lengths to read secrets. The British in 1540 established three agencies – the Secret Office, Deciphering Office, and Private Office – to open suspicious mail, crack the codes or ciphers, and then reseal and deliver the notes. These spies discovered Mary, Queen of Scots, was considering Queen Elizabeth's assassination, a revelation that quickly led to Mary's own beheading.

Francis Bacon in the 1620's devised a particularly sophisticated cipher consisting only of the letters "a" and "b," not unlike the "0"s and "1"s used by modern computers. As noted before, this biliteral alphabet had "A" represented by "aaaaa," while "B" would be "aaaab," and so on. Bacon further disguised his messages by using different type faces, so italicized letters would be the "a"s while regular type would represent "b"s.

World War I brought cryptography to a new level, with changes as profound as that conflict's more acknowledged revolutions in weaponry. The portable machine gun, for example, allowed mass killings, replacing the concepts of honor and glory that had been associated with traditional warfare's direct and individualized conflict. The multiple-firing weapon, said one historian, "negated all the old human virtues – pluck, fortitude, patriotism, honor – and made them as nothing in the face of a deadly stream of bullets."[187] Germany held a clear armaments advantage with more than 5,000 machine guns compared to less than 300 for the British, whose soldiers gallantly mounted their horses and flashed their sabers only to meet a rain of destruction. "When we started to fire we just had to load and reload," a German machine gunner later wrote. "They went down in the hundreds. We didn't have to aim, we just fired into them."[188]

Death in warfare had become mechanized. In this conflict, according to another historian, "Scientists, engineers, and mechanics would be as important as soldiers."[189] The same could be said for code breakers.

Although armies had long connived to learn their enemy's plans, technological advancements in the early 20th century, particularly cipher machines and radios, increased the value of intelligence gathering and moved cryptology increasingly from the field to the laboratory. Decipherment focused less on coded words and more on the precise placement of individual letters, causing it to shift from linguists to mathematicians.

Radio broadcasts, meanwhile, allowed commanders to enjoy direct and rapid communication with their troops, a genuine improvement over the telegraph or telephone lines that often could not be strung to frontline positions. Such radio transmissions, however, could be intercepted by virtually anyone with a receiver, so the challenge became to encode (and decode) this ever expanding traffic of messages.

Cryptology during the early telegraph years, wrote historian David Kahn, "was interesting but inconsequential, intriguing but academic." Yet when World War I commanders could obtain a constant stream of intercepts, code breaking became "a weapon, a pursuit entailing all the savagery of warfare and life against death."[190]

The changing attitude toward intelligence gathering matched in many ways the ideological shift from noble battles based on individual courage to mass death caused by advanced machines. Great War combatants slowly abandoned their "honorable" code that "gentlemen did not read each others' mail" as they sought sophisticated means to intercept and decipher their enemy's messages.

World War I

The British by 1914 might have produced few machine guns, but they were far ahead of the Germans in the craft of codes and ciphers – an advantage that resulted from both luck and skill. England's initial stroke of fortune appeared in early September when Russians picked up in the Baltic Sea a drowned German officer from the wrecked light cruiser *Magdeburg*. "Clasped in his bosom by arms rigid in death were the cypher and signal books of the German Navy and the minutely squared maps of the North Sea and the Heligoland Bight," wrote Winston Churchill, then First Lord of the Admiralty. "The Russians (who were allies of the English against the Germans) felt that as the leading naval Power, the British Admiralty ought to have these books and charts."[191]

The skill part resulted largely from Alfred Ewing, whose official title as director of naval education masked a brilliant scientist who recently had been knighted for his insights on mechanical engineering and magnetism. Ewing would become president of the British Association for the Advancement of Science, yet in 1914 he appeared to be the only person in the Admiralty interested in cryptology. Sensing a pressing need for military intelligence, he quickly consulted experts from numerous colleges, read code books stored at Lloyd's of London and the General Post Office, and assembled a team of bright young men, many of whom had attended the elite Eton College. Yet even with knowledge of Germany's four-letter codes from the *Magdeburg* book, that team needed some three weeks to crack the mono-alphabetic substitution contained within the enemy's naval messages.

Ewing's operation, however, improved rapidly. Known as "Room 40" because of its location within the Old Buildings of the Admiralty, the team became "so proficient that the new key (to the code, which the Germans broadcast to their offices each day at midnight) was sometimes solved as early as 2 or 3 a.m. and nearly always by 9 or 10 a.m."[192] The team, it was later estimated, intercepted and interpreted almost 15,000 of Germany's secret messages.

The British, meanwhile, developed their own two-part "Cypher SA" that was considered "unquestionably the era's finest code," largely because of its extensive use of the polyphone that allowed for different translations.[193] As explained by historian David Kahn, "Obviously, if codegroup 07640 can mean either *eight*, or *fifth April*, or *then North-ward*, the task of the cryptanalyst becomes substantially more difficult."[194]

Britain's intelligence lead offered clear advantages on the battlefield and high seas. According to Churchill, "Without the cryptographers' department there would have been no Battle of Jutland," where English battleships boxed in Berlin's fleet for the rest of the war.[195] As a result, Britain's coastal communities were spared regular bombardment from German naval artillery.

While England shared little intelligence with her allies, the French independently advanced the art and science of code-breaking. Their master cryptographer was Captain Georges Painvin, a brilliant intellect who taught paleontology, won music contests on his cello, but perhaps is best known for his role in capturing Mata Hari.

That task required deciphering the highly secret diplomatic messages between Germany and Spain, which included radioed pleas by the German naval attaché based in Madrid for Berlin to send money and instructions for agent "H-21." That German spy was a stunning exotic dancer and courtesan who maintained relationships with numerous Allied politicians and high-ranking military officers. Born in the Netherlands as Margaretha Geertruida Zelle, she learned sacred Hindu dances in Indonesia before moving to Paris, where she initially rode circus horses and then acted at the Musee Guimet. The French accused Mata Hari of the spying that caused the deaths of at least 50,000 soldiers. While she argued the German funds delivered to her accounts were nothing more than gifts from her many lovers, the Paris court paid more attention to Painvin's translations of damning

119

messages and sentenced Mata Hari to death by a twelve-man firing squad, before which she refused a blindfold. (Greta Garbo stared in a 1931 movie based loosely on the dancer's life and exploits.)

Even more consequential was Britain's interception of a message from Arthur Zimmerman, the German Foreign Minister, to his ambassador in Mexico. To set the context, consider that the futile slaughter of trench warfare had caused immense suffering for both the Allies and Germany. Britain and France desperately wanted the United States to join the fight and break the stalemate, but President Woodrow Wilson had just won reelection with the slogan "He kept us out of war." Germany, meanwhile, sought to blockade Britain but feared the aggressive use of submarines might hurt U.S. shippers and port workers, tipping America's attitude towards war.

So when Room 40 intercepted the Zimmerman telegram suggesting a German military alliance with Mexico, the code breakers realized they possessed the ammunition that could force the U.S. to join the conflict. The message, indeed, was incendiary as it baldly declared Germany's intention to launch "unrestricted submarine warfare" that "offers the prospect of compelling England in a few months to make peace." More troubling for the U.S., the telegram offered Mexico a deal – join the war effort with Germany and "reconquer the lost territory in Texas, New Mexico, and Arizona."[196]

The valuable message, however, presented British diplomats with a problem. Revealing the translation no doubt would stir American public opinion but it also would disclose one of England's best-kept secrets – its ability to decipher German communications, a realization that would prompt Berlin to change substantially its codes and ciphers. Since the Zimmerman telegram had been sent via "neutral" Sweden, exposure also would stir Americans to wonder if the British were capturing and reading their messages, too. Eventually, however, London took its chances and shared the news with American officials.

The story blazed from eight-column headlines in U.S. newspapers on March 1, 1917. While some anti-war activists doubted the telegram's authenticity and asserted it was nothing more than a British fabrication designed to move U.S. public opinion, most Americans did not take kindly to Germany's plan to give away a chunk of the United States. Wilson, who three months before had declared that entering the war would be a "crime against civilization," traveled to Capitol Hill on April 2 to ask Congress for the funds needed to make the world "safe for democracy." "That it (the German government) means to stir up enemies against us at our very doors, the intercepted note to the German minister at Mexico City is eloquent evidence," the president declared. "We are accepting this challenge of hostile purpose."[197]

"No other single cryptanalysis has had such enormous consequences," wrote historian David Kahn. "Never before or since has so much turned upon the solution of a secret message."[198] Room 40's actions quite simply spurred the United States to declare war, enabling the allies to win.

The United States, at the time, had nothing to compare to Britain's cryptographic capacity. It did, however, have George Fabyan.

In part to demonstrate London's cryptographic dominance and in part to test its latest cipher machine, the British Army asked the American military if it could translate a half dozen of England's secret messages. British Captain St. Vincent Plett had cleverly added two circles of letters, one containing 27 intervals and the other 26, to an existing cryptograph, supposedly making the resulting ciphers unbreakable. The British Army claimed "the solution of messages sent by it is possible only with a great many messages and that so long a time will be required that messages will lose their value before solution."[199] Feeling a bit arrogant, England's code-makers claimed their only fear was the Germans might capture the cryptograph machine and "we would be unable to read their messages."

Washington officials accepted London's challenge, but, lacking their own cryptanalysts, turned to the patriotic colonel and his Riverbank colleagues, who were happy to make a transition from literary to military codes. "It looked like an insurmountable task," wrote Elizabeth Friedman.

GEORGE FABYAN

"A field cipher, used in war, would be utilized a hundred or two hundred times a day, and even if the key were changed every day, there would be a great mass of messages to study. But here we had six short messages, and we were dealing with two alphabets, one moving irregularly against the other and we had no knowledge of either."[200]

William Friedman made the reasoned – or intuitive or lucky, depending upon your view about the role of science, art, or chance in cryptanalysis – assumption the London-based sender had used "cipher" as a key word and a related word would be in the second alphabet. He tried several combinations – including "cipher method" and "cipher solution" – but none worked. He turned to Elizabeth, who later wrote: "I was sitting across the room from him, busily engaged on another message. He asked me to lean back in my chair, close my eyes and make my mind blank, at least as blank as possible. Then he would ask me a question. I was not to consider the reply even for a second but just give the word which his question brought to my mind. I did as he said. He spoke the word 'cipher' and I instantly replied, 'machine.' A few minutes later he said the answer was right."

Within a few hours, the Friedmans deciphered all six messages, the first one of which declared boldly: "This message is absolutely indecipherable." They wired that very message back to Washington, prompting the director of Army Intelligence to telegraph London: "Please inform Captain Hay of British Military Intelligence that messages enciphered by Plett's machine have been broken by method of attack different from any considered by inventor, and that system is considered dangerous in presence of enemy."[201]

London quickly got over its bruised ego because Scotland Yard needed help stopping a German plot to help Indian nationalists break away from England, or at least to divert British attention from the western front. Concerned that Hindu spies and terrorists were raising funds and purchasing weapons in the United States, British officials delivered to Fabyan and the Friedmans an attaché case packed with intercepted letters.

122

Many of the messages contained clusters of three numbers, which the code-breakers assumed referred to words in a dictionary held by both the senders and recipients. The first digit, they deduced, pointed to the page in the dictionary, the second to that page's first or second column, while the final number to the word. By trial and error, they decided "99-2-14" – the 14th word in the second column of the 99th page – was "you." From there, concluded Friedman, "The code number 99-2-17, which may occur several times, must represent a word, certainly not far from 'you,' and since there are but two or three relatively uncommon words ('young,' 'youth,' etc.) intervening between 'you' and 'your,' the word is probably 'your.'"[202]

Such logic highlights Friedman's frequent use of the frequency principle, which recognizes certain words – "the," "of," "and," and "to" – appear most regularly in English writing. That principle also calculates words starting with "a" account for 6.43 percent of English terms while 5.25 percent begin with "b," thereby allowing cryptographers to increase their odds that certain translated words begin with certain letters. (Riverbank researchers devised similar ratios for other languages.)

Using these tactics and without ever seeing the actual dictionary, the Friedmans deciphered virtually every word of the confiscated letters, enough so police could round up 135 Indian plotters. When William and Elizabeth in December 1917 arrived in San Francisco to provide expert testimony at the terrorist trial, they happened into a bookstore adjacent to the University of California in Berkeley. After hearing of the Friedmans' project, an elderly employee rummaged through the stacks and found an 1880 edition of a German-English dictionary, which proved to be the Hindus' code book.

The Friedmans delivered incriminating testimony of the German-Indian plot, revealing the conspirators' detailed plans in their own words. Already sensational, the trial gained national notoriety because one of the conspirators, Ram Singh, entered the courtroom with a revolver hidden under his robe. When Ram Chandra – perhaps America's best-known Hindu who had turned state's evidence – took the witness stand and began to testify, the terrorist stood up and shot him. A federal marshal at the back of the courtroom quickly leveled his weapon and killed the murderer. The next day, the jury found all the surviving plotters guilty.

Fabyan offered the services of the Friedmans and their Riverbank colleagues to the U.S. military, and the millionaire noted there would be no charge. "I was wondering if the information which I had in reference to these ciphers would be of any use to the Government," he wrote.[203]

Washington was in no position to reject such help since U.S. forces knowledgeable of ciphers were limited to three individuals and since the security of America's own codes was almost laughable. The War Department's Telegraph Code, in fact, was published by a Cleveland-based commercial printer with no security clearance, and London officials regularly informed their Washington counterparts U.S. messages were easily read.

Colonel J.O. Mauborgne, who was to become director of the U.S. Signal Corps, visited Riverbank in mid April 1917, clearly looking for help translating Germany's increased volume of encoded letters. Mauborgne paid particular attention to Fabyan's security, evaluating the presence of vaults, fire protection, and patrols. He wrote back to his superiors: "The intelligence division of the General Staff, like the Department of Justice, is urged to take immediate advantage of Colonel Fabyan's offer to decipher captured messages."

Before their success with the Hindu plotters, most of the Friedmans' cryptographic efforts at Riverbank had been limited to finding secret messages within Shakespeare's texts. "We had a lot of pioneering to do," admitted Elizabeth. "Literary ciphers may give you the swing of the thing, but they were in no sense scientific. There were no precedents for us to follow. We simply had to roll up our sleeves and chart a new course. We, therefore, became the learners or students and the teachers and workers all at once, at the same time."[204]

While Mrs. Gallup took her Bacon-Shakespeare efforts to another portion of the estate, Fabyan and the Friedmans hired 17 cryptanalysts to focus on government work for the Army, Department of Justice, State

Department, Post Office, and several other agencies. Since many of the initial intercepts were of messages between Germany's headquarters and its Mexican ambassador, Fabyan also hired several German and Spanish linguists. "We turned out an enormous amount of work," said Elizebeth.[205]

The U.S. government, according to William Friedman, intercepted messages "by various and entirely surreptitious means from telegraphs and cable offices in Washington and elsewhere in the U.S." Washington typically mailed the notes to Riverbank, but a few highly sensitive texts – and their solutions – were telegraphed back and forth.

Perhaps as important as decoding messages, Fabyan and the Friedmans trained the personnel who would staff the newly formed Cipher Bureau within Military Intelligence, what became known as Military Intelligence 8 (or MI-8). Almost eighty officers – most of whom would later be sent to General Pershing's headquarters in France – arrived at Riverbank in October 1917 and were housed at the nearby Aurora Hotel. Although Fabyan treated them to fine meals and wines, they endured a six-week crash course on cryptanalysis under the strict tutelage of William Friedman, who had developed a curriculum of pamphlets and worksheets.

The first Friedman publication, *A Method of Reconstructing the Primary Alphabet from a Single One of the Series of Secondary Alphabets*, explained spatial relationship among the letters of a coded alphabet. He wrote seven other papers, one with Elizebeth. Combined, the reports represented the first texts associated with the science of cryptanalysis, providing a mathematical foundation to this fast-evolving field.

Some of the publications were basic tutorials for the assembled Army officers. "Deciphering," wrote Friedman in his *Introduction to Methods for the Solution of Ciphers*, "is both a science and an art. It is a science because certain definite laws and principles have been established which pertain to it; it is also an art because of the large part played in it by imagination, skill, and experience. Yet it may be said that in no other science are the rules and principles so little followed and so often broken; and in no other art is the part played by reasoning and logic so great."[206]

GEORGE FABYAN

A good decipherer, explained Friedman, is "able to modify his methods and discard his assumptions." Yet he admitted the mind's greatest ally "is that indefinable, intangible something, which we would forever pursue if we could – luck."[207]

The instructor also demanded specific habits. Work sheets, for instance, "SHOULD NOT BE DESTROYED" because they offer a record of the cryptanalytic efforts. Soft lead pencils should be utilized since they allow erasures. Finally, decipherers should not work alone since "a group of two operators, working harmoniously as a unit, can accomplish more than four operators working singly."[208]

Perhaps Friedman's most significant intellectual contribution was *The Index of Coincidence and Its Applications in Cryptography*, which was divided into two parts, the first showing "how a cipher system involving more than one hundred unknown, random mixed alphabets can be solved without necessitating a single assumption of plain text values." The second portion demonstrated "how a multiple alphabet cipher system, involving both substitution and transposition processes in a somewhat complicated method, can be solved from a single message of no great length."[209]

On graduation day for his code-breaking cadets, the colonel assembled the group in two rows outside the Aurora Hotel. At first glance, the resulting photograph appears to be a straightforward shot of the 76 officers and associated Riverbank staff. Yet a closer look reveals some of the men faced the camera while others looked to the left. They formed, in fact, a Baconian biliteral cipher. Those facing forward represented "a"s while those looking sideways were the "b"s. Reading from left to right, the first five figures spelt out the letter "k," and the entire group revealed the colonel's favorite axiom from Sir Francis Bacon: "Knowledge is power."

The cipher was not perfect, in part because the group was four short of the number needed to complete the final "r" and in part because one soldier looked the wrong way. Still, Friedman throughout his career kept a copy of the treasured photograph under a glass plate covering his desk, as well as a larger framed version on the wall of his study. It reminded him how cryptography allowed him to make anything signify anything.

When not teaching, the Friedmans and Fabyan focused on practical problems, such as proving the vulnerability of the U.S. Army's basic field cipher. The running assumption had been such ciphers based on "running keys" could not be deciphered, yet the Friedmans felt "it is altogether probable that the enemy, who has been preparing for war for a long time, has not neglected to look into our field ciphers, and we are inclined to credit him with a knowledge equal to or superior to our own." The Riverbank team tinkered for weeks and, to the shock of MI-8, eventually concluded: "We have been able to prove that not only is a single short message enciphered by the U.S. Army Disk, or any similar device, easily and quickly deciphered, but that a series of messages sent out in the same key may be deciphered more rapidly than they have been enciphered!"[210]

Because of these activities and accomplishments, Friedman was in demand by the U.S. government. That fact worried Fabyan. When the colonel heard Friedman might be called up, he pleaded with his Washington contacts to have the code breaker remain at Riverbank, even if he became a commissioned officer. Have him, requested Fabyan "stay here and be loaned to such duties as may appear to be in the best interests of the Government."[211]

Washington, however, tried to go around the colonel and reach out directly to Friedman, yet the code breaker never received those letters because Fabyan had the invasive habit of opening mail addressed to his staff. The result was a delay that postponed Friedman's commissioning, allowing him only five months with General Pershing's headquarters.

Friedman's time in France, although short, proved to be quite productive. He reported for duty in Chaumont, having been assigned to the Radio Intelligence Section within Military Intelligence, where his job, put simply, was to learn Germany's secrets. Friedman chose to work on codes rather than ciphers even though he had considerable experience with the latter and none with the former. His choice reflected a desire "to broaden my professional knowledge and practice in cryptology," and he later concluded, "Little did I realize what a painful and frustrating period of learning and training I had undertaken, but my choice turned out to be a very wise and useful one."[212]

His first success came in early March 1918 as the Germans planned their last great offensive. To coordinate the planning, Berlin devised a new "Schluesselheft" code, known to the Allies as the "three-number code." Fortunately for Friedman, German field commanders lacked familiarity with their own code and regularly returned messages with the letters "OS," an abbreviation for "ohne Sinn," or "message unintelligible." This response forced German headquarters to resend the messages, both in the new Schluesselheft as well as the previous version. Little did Berlin know that Americans intercepting the messages already had broken the earlier code, and, thus, were able to decipher Schlusselheft and alert American commanders to Germany's plans. After the war, Colonel Frank Moorman, chief of the Radio Intelligence Section, said cracking Schluesselheft "must certainly have cost the lives of thousands of Germans and conceivably it changed the result of one of the greatest efforts made by the German armies."[213]

For the same March 1918 offensive, Berlin also introduced the ADFGVX cipher to be used for important messages among the German High Command. Those messages were hard to translate, in part because of the relatively few transmissions, but also because of the cipher's complexity, involving, in the words of cryptanalysts, a division, a substitution, as well as a transposition. Most credit for finding a solution went to French Captain Georges Painvin, although Friedman devised the mechanical solution for translating messages containing similar endings.

In addition to Painvin, the era's other cryptographic giants included Herbert Yardley (head of the cryptologic section of the Military Intelligence Division, MI-8), Parker Hitt (author of the *Manual for the*

Solution of Military Ciphers), and Joseph Mauborgne (Chief Signal Officer beginning in 1937). Yet according to the key historian of code breakers, "Unquestionably the greatest is William Frederick Friedman."[214]

Lieutenant Colonel Friedman after the war was directed to write "Field Codes Used by the German Army during the World War." In addition to reviewing German and American efforts, he expanded on his thoughts about the integration of art and science in cryptography: "It should be noted that in this whole process the part played by chance, by the happy coincidences which were always lurking everywhere for the watchful eye of the worker to note, by the mistakes of a foolish or a careless encoder, and by a fortunate 'long shot' or guess by the decoder, cannot be overestimated. Often the minutest and most insignificant of clues formed the starting point for the unraveling of a whole chain of groups."[215]

Yet beyond paying tribute to the Allies' instincts and intelligence, Friedman virtually mocked Berlin's encoders for their "unintelligent pedantry." Of great assistance to American decoders, for instance, was the German habit of using the same punctuation in its coded messages as in the plaintext. In addition, said Friedman, "The fact that the Germans had a predilection for repeating certain proverbs many times caused the establishment of a single letter often to result in locating these proverbs and thus, in turn, the solution of a whole series of important spelling groups in a new code was effected."[216]

Options

After completing his military paperwork, Friedman confronted career choices. Should he stay in the Army, perhaps to help establish a permanent cryptography office in Washington? Should he return to genetics, his original love? Should he go back to Riverbank, in part to further study the writings of Sir Francis Bacon?

Fabyan frequently appealed for the code breaker's return, but Friedman increasingly offered curt rebukes, in large part because he had learned of the colonel's deceit in opening his mail and postponing his military commissioning. According to a friend, Friendman "feels he missed one of the big opportunities of his life by not being commissioned in 1917, for had he been sent to France at that time he would have had an opportunity to make a name for himself."[217] The code breaker eventually wrote a scathing five-page letter to Fabyan that revealed the complexities of their relationship. Angry he would have been one rank higher and wealthier if he had joined the Army early, Friedman questioned the colonel's "motives of private interest" that led him to confiscate the government's offers, yet he concluded Fabyan probably was "acting from motives of what one may call 'paternalism.'" Yet, Friedman continued, "The fact remains that (Elizebeth and I) are, in your own language, 'free, white, and twenty-one.' We had a right to know and to be allowed to judge for ourselves."

Another source of tension was Fabyan's decision to publish Friedman's *The Index of Coincidence* in Paris by the Imprimerie-Librairie Militaire Universelle as a 87-page brochure, but without giving any credit to Friedman or Riverbank Laboratories. The colonel, in fact, copyrighted each Riverbank publication and typically printed only 200 copies. According to Friedman, "Since he paid for their production, Colonel Fabyan exercised careful control over their distribution, presenting copies to students and friends as the spirit moved him." Much to the code breaker's disappointment, Fabyan "withheld copies even from the author, save for an extremely limited number, in one case the author receiving but two copies."[218]

In addition to attacking Fabyan for opening his mail and restricting his access to publications, Friedman criticized the colonel's autocratic ways of running the laboratories: "Honesty prompts me to say that in my opinion your judgment of human nature and ability along academic lines will have to undergo severe changes to enable you to make a success of academic activities, as you have of business activities."[219] Friedman also mocked Fabyan's promotion of nonexistent biliteral ciphers within Shakespeare's plays and poems, and he accused the colonel of favoring salesmanship over scholarship: "You cannot force those whose word the academic world respects and accepts to believe the existence of a thing you are trying to prove by advertising methods."[220]

Fabyan did not respond to the various charges. Instead, he offered a curt business reply: "The facts in the case are that you are practically loaned for the (war) emergency. The emergency no longer exists and in justice to yourself, your own future, and myself, I think the sooner you return to Riverbank the better."[221]

With William in France, Elizebeth had left Fabyan's estate in the fall of 1918, moving back to her family home in Huntington, Indiana, ostensibly to care for her sick father. The departure, however, had more to do with her growing anger towards the colonel and her discontent with conditions at Riverbank. According to William, Elizebeth was "exceedingly embittered" by Fabyan's actions and "absolutely opposed" to returning to Chicago.[222] The feelings appeared to be mutual. "The colonel hated her most fervently," stated William, "because she saw through him and his wiles very early in the game."[223]

Fabyan, however, tried to soften up Elizebeth in order to regain William's services. In a personal letter to her, he tried to explain that some conditions associated with her discontent were beyond his control and others had been eliminated. "I make mistakes the same as others," the colonel admitted, "but I think, even you will admit, they are of the head rather than the heart."[224] Fabyan even wrote to William that "Elizebeth has made a mistake in leaving Riverbank. There are many opportunities which come up there and if a person is there they are in a position to take advantage of the opportunity."[225]

The Friedmans slowly realized their opportunities were diminishing since William had spent months unsuccessfully trying to find employment in the genetics industry. "When I arrived from France," he wrote, "my mind was fully made up to go into business. After looking around for a considerable length of time, and conferring with friends, it seemed inadvisable to do so just at present on account of unsettled business conditions."[226]

Friedman's government overtures proved equally frustrating. Most troubling, he failed an army medical exam, without the benefit of appeal, because of a so-called heart condition. Only several years later did Friedman discover the medical board's chairman was Fabyan's brother-in-law. Although the colonel's interference was indirect at best, Friedman came to feel Fabyan kept him from further military employment by encouraging undue concern about a minor ailment.[227] Fabyan letters also mysteriously arrived at the industrial companies where Friedman was interviewing for a job. "We had the feeling the colonel was stalking us," complained Elizebeth.[228]

Fabyan, meanwhile, cabled Friedman several times with a generous offer: "Your salary has been going on."[229] Running low on cash and options, William and Elizebeth relented but set strict conditions on any Riverbank return. They adamantly refused to live at the estate, preferring instead to rent a small house in nearby Geneva. They declared their names must appear on any document they wrote, and they demanded complete freedom to determine if Bacon was the true Shakespeare. The colonel finally agreed, and the Friedmans returned in the summer of 1919.

The colonel did try to be endearing, in part by giving to the Friedmans a rare book on ciphers, published in the 1600's and valued at about $3,000. "It was the only time Fabyan ever gave something to anyone," said Elizebeth cynically. "He usually extracted from everyone."

William, however, did not want to close the door on future Riverbank opportunities. "We both know that during my three years at Riverbank we never had any serious differences, that I can recall at least," wrote the code breaker to the colonel. "If it were not for the fact that I like to work with you and for you, that there are certain advantages to be had at Riverbank that do not obtain elsewhere." In fact, Friedman continued, "Our relations have been more than those of employer and employee."[230]

Yet despite such generous tokens and kind words, the relationship did not improve. Fabyan continued to press the significance of Bacon's biliteral ciphers, and he couldn't contain his habit of barking directives about his team's professional and personal lives. He also failed to provide any of William's promised back salary.

Still, the colonel and the Friedmans worked together closely, most prominently on Fabyan's dispute with the War Department about the security of AT&T's encipherment system, which for more than a year had been transmitting sensitive government and business messages. The colonel during the war had visited the company's New York facility and abruptly pronounced its cipher could be broken. With Friedman in Europe, he and other Riverbank staff tried to crack the messages but met only failure after failure. Still, the ever-confident colonel in March 1919 wrote again to AT&T, "I am still of the opinion that the cipher is breakable, although it has cost me several thousand dollars to confirm my off-hand opinion expressed in your office."[231]

The War Department disagreed and began to think Fabyan was wasting his money and their time, and maybe even losing his sanity. General Marlborough Churchill, director of Military Intelligence, went so far as to declare the AT&T system is "considered by this office to be absolutely indecipherable."[232]

Churchill basically challenged Fabyan to put up or shut up, and he forwarded 50 AT&T transmitted messages to Riverbank in October 1919. Friedman, now back from France, spent six weeks of 12-hour days trying to complete the translations. He neared the point of complete exhaustion when an assistant accidently discovered the Riverbank team had mistakenly omitted a character from the cipher tapes. That realization offered Friedman his first clue to the plaintext, and by December 8 he had translated all the messages. "In order to prove that this was true," wrote Friedman, "I sent a perforated cipher-message tape to each of the (Army) officers involved. In order to decipher these messages the chief signal officer had to use his own key tapes which had been employed in enciphering the challenge messages, so that Riverbank was in a position to produce the plaintext of any of the latter on request, if further proof of solution was needed or desired."[233]

Embarrassed, General Churchill abandoned the AT&T program and apologized. "Your very brilliant scientific achievement reflects great credit upon you and your whole personnel," he wrote to Colonel Fabyan. "It would be impossible to exaggerate in paying you and Riverbank the deserved tribute for this very scholarly accomplishment."[234]

Government officials, as a result, appealed again for Friedman to move to Washington, and they found a way around the medical board's rejection. The Signal Corps' Major Mauborgne wrote, "We need your services with the Government. ...We feel that it would be a great misfortune if the Friedman family were to retire to some other kind of a job than code and cipher work and hope to make an arrangement which is agreeable to both you and ourselves."[235]

Negotiations, however, were contentious. Friedman initially suggested $3,000 a year and an Army commission as first lieutenant, while Elizebeth would be paid $1,520 annually. Yet when Washington presented a counter offer, he telegraphed his "serious disappointment. Could not possibly accept lieutenancy. Might consider captaincy. ... Feel my experience and ability of considerable value to Signal Corps and certainly worth more than lieutenancy."[236]

Discussions were kept secret, largely because of Fabyan's past practice of intercepting letters and appealing to his Washington contacts. Worried "the old gentleman seems to be smelling a rat," Friedman wrote to military officials, "I am fully convinced that should he really find out our plans before the time is ripe, he would stop at almost nothing to prevent their consummation."[237]

Fabyan, in fact, did hear of the plans and confronted the Friedmans, promising to double the government's salary offer if they remained at Riverbank. The Friedmans "then stayed on a little while, but no raise in salary was ever forthcoming," complained Elizebeth. "It happened twice."[238]

The code breakers finally agreed to begin in Washington, D.C., on January 1, 1921, as civilian cryptographers for the U.S. Army's Black Chamber. Fearing last-minute tactics by the colonel, William and Elizebeth showed up at the Riverbank laboratories on the morning of their departure dressed in traveling clothes. William later acknowledged the colonel accepted their decision with "good grace."

The Friedmans greatly enjoyed their move to the nation's capital, where they rented a small apartment on Connecticut Avenue. Elizebeth savored Washington's four theatres, which they attended a couple of times a week, when they were not hosting tennis parties, barbeques, and concerts. "We formed a music group," boasted Elizebeth. "General Mauborgne – as he was to become – played the violin, as did William Friedman. I played the piano, a friend we had known in Geneva, Illinois, played the cello, and a friend in the Army played the fourth instrument in the quartet. When the windows were open in the summer we used to have crowds listening in the street below."[239]

They also enjoyed being away from Colonel Fabyan. "Everything is fine down here," William wrote to a Riverbank friend. "Like the work and the people very much. A great deal more to live for, and many more friends, and things to do. And Freedom – oh! Boy. Toward the last out there in Geneva it would not have taken much persuasion to have shuffled off. But it's all over now."[240]

Although the Friedmans found their initial assignments to be "very interesting and useful," those tasks tended to be the routine development of low-level codes. Yet William in 1922 was promoted to direct the Black Chamber's Research and Development Division, and a few years later became the War Department's chief cryptanalyst, a position he held for the next 25 years. Despite these growing responsibilities, Friedman took it as a personal slight that the Army offered so little financial support after World War I to cryptography, particularly since he and his small team were overwhelmed by a growing avalanche of messages intercepted by the War and Justice Departments.

Friedman, however, relished the work. According to Elizebeth, "He could not tolerate not being busy every minute." A strict and aloof manager, he became admired by his colleagues, who envied his cryptographic talents and declared him to be like Midas because "everything he touched turned into plaintext."[241]

The work included diverse assignments. Senator Thomas J. Walsh, the leading Democrat on a congressional investigative subcommittee, called upon Friedman in 1924 to help decode messages that would prove the U.S. Secretary of the Interior, Albert Fall, had sold government property – including Wyoming's oil-rich Teapot Dome – at bargain-basement prices to bribing petroleum marketers. Fall, who served in the cabinet of President Warren Harding, had leased the fields, without competitive bidding, to Sinclair Oil's Harry Sinclair, who offered gifts to Fall totaling what today would be more than $4 million.

The leases themselves were not illegal since Sinclair and other oilmen had convinced Congress that private petroleum companies could better manage government-owned petroleum deposits reserved for emergency use by the U.S. Navy. The gifts were another matter, and Fall and Sinclair went out of their ways to stifle Walsh's investigation, destroying hundreds of records and even ransacking the offices of Senator Robert LaFollette, the Republican committee chairman. Although suspicious of Secretary Fall's lucrative business investments and elaborate improvements to his cattle ranch, Senator Walsh struggled for more than two years to find convincing evidence of kickbacks. Finally, with Friedman's help, he discovered and translated coded messages about a large, no-interest loan from Sinclair to Fall.

Friedman received national publicity for providing the congressional investigative panel with crucial evidence, but he privately admitted "the decoding of those messages was certainly no remarkable feat, nor was it even one calling for any skill beyond the average code clerk."[242] After several hours trying to break down the conspirators' messages through a variety of mathematical processes, he realized the notes simply had been written with a code book used by Justice Department agents. By walking over to that agency and obtaining the volume, the dispatches, he said, "were not 'broken' – they were merely 'read.'" Secretary Fall in 1929 was found guilty of bribery and sentenced to a year in prison, becoming the first cabinet member to be incarcerated for his actions in office. Two others within President Harding's inner circle subsequently were forced to resign. Sinclair was charged with contempt and a fine for not cooperating with government investigators, and he received a short prison sentence for jury tampering.

The Coast Guard, meanwhile, recruited Elizebeth to help catch narcotics and liquor smugglers. She became a "special agent" responsible for the counter-intelligence campaigns that deciphered and decoded the criminals' messages.

On one of her first assignments, she obtained evidence against the West Coast's most ruthless drug runners. The Coast Guard had intercepted one of the gang's letters, posted in Shanghai, that appeared to contain nothing but gibberish, with letter sequences such as "wyrras" and "wysats." Elizebeth, however, quickly recognized the use of a double-code system and sent back to the Coast Guard the hidden message: "Our shipment goes today. It consists of 520 tins of smoking opium and 20 tins sample, 70 ounces cocaine, 70 ounces morphine, 40 ounces heroin."[243]

Still needed, of course, was hard evidence linking the smugglers to the actual drugs. That came four days later when Elizebeth decoded a second message about the criminals' plans to deliver the narcotics at San Francisco's docks in eight numbered drums of tung oil aboard the *Asama Maru*. With that information, Coast Guard agents confronted the Japanese merchant ship when it arrived in California, and the drug smugglers received the maximum sentence of 12 years.

Elizebeth also found herself testifying at several liquor-running trials during Prohibition. One defense lawyer tried to discredit Friedman's work, arguing she could not prove his clients' code word for "alcohol" did not mean "walnuts" or "apples." Elizebeth calmly turned to the judge and asked, "Your Honor, is there a blackboard available to the Court?" She then spent the next hour, according to a newspaper account, providing "a courtroom class in Cryptography." The impressed judge pronounced the liquor runners guilty.

GEORGE FABYAN

Yet perhaps her most publicized case involved a two-masted schooner, named *I'm Alone*, the Coast Guard believed was transporting alcohol illegally from Belize to New Orleans. When the Canadian-registered vessel refused to stop and be searched, the Coast Guard fired several warning shots across its bow, and when the vessel kept sailing the Americans sent live ammo below the schooner's water line. Canadian officials did not appreciate one of their vessels being sunk on the high seas, and they demanded formal apologies and compensation for the damages. Elizabeth's task was to decipher messages between the schooner and a well-known rumrunner in order to prove the vessel actually was controlled by Americans who were breaking U.S. Prohibition laws.

Supreme Court justices in both the United States and Canada tried to resolve the diplomatic dispute. The schooner's captain admitted to running rum but claimed he was more than 12 miles from the United States and in international waters when the Coast Guard first approached. Providing color to the case, he declared, "I didn't give a tinker's cuss where the liquor went after I was through with it."[244]

The dispute turned violent when the vessel's owner – Dan Hogan, known as the Al Capone of Louisiana and head of a $15-million smuggling syndicate – murdered one of the witnesses and even threatened Elizebeth, who, without her knowledge, obtained an armed Justice Department detail to protect her. Yet Friedman's testimony at the 1933 trial in New Orleans eventually led to the alcohol trafficker's conviction, breaking up the Prohibition era's largest and most powerful bootlegging ring and ending what had become an international incident.

Everything seemed to be well with the Friedmans. Daughter Barbara found William to be an "attentive, witty, and generous father." Friends enjoyed his affable ways, and colleagues appreciated their punctual, dapper, and rather formal leader. One associate in private affectionately called him "Uncle Willie," yet at a social party "when the two of us were by ourselves and I called him 'Uncle Willie,' I was immediately made aware of my impertinence. One did not take liberties with William F. Friedman."[245]

Everyone enjoyed Friedman's good-hearted passion for cryptology. The children played "The Game of Secrecy," a series of coded tests developed by their father, and the family's Christmas cards featured cipher messages. Friends, moreover, were treated to progressive dinner parties where guests received from the first restaurant owner "a piece of paper containing a clue about the next place to go. They'd go to five or six restaurants. ... The first team to return home won a prize."[246]

William certainly kept busy, playing tennis most Sunday mornings and enjoying periodic rounds of golf. With an extensive set of tools, he also built an attic work-room for his son and a swimming pool for his wife.

William and Elizebeth, according to friends, enjoyed a loving relationship. He regularly sent to her Talisman roses, one for each year of marriage. They frequently cooperated on joint projects, although they studiously avoided discussing each others' secret work.

Yet few recognized William was an overworked, stressed, and depressed individual who began seeing a psychoanalyst in 1927, and who in January 1941 entered Walter Reed Army Medical Center's psychiatric ward complaining of severe depression and nervous fatigue. Friedman's outgoing ways masked secret anxieties – worries about finances, coping with being a Jew in WASPy Washington, and hiding the particulars of his covert assignments from friends and family.[247]

Friedman and Fabyan maintained regular, if rancorous, contact. The code breaker kept the colonel apprised of his Washington-based efforts, such as his more efficient method of preparing codes, which, Friedman argued, reduced the encoder's time requirements by 75 percent. The colonel, in turn, often asked Friedman for advice, such as on his idea for a telegraph that would "handle the message by a ray of light projected on a film making an undulating wave which, on being fed through the machine, will be translated by vibrations into a horn audible to the ear."[248]

GEORGE FABYAN

Fabyan addressed most of his letters to "Billy," and he frequently praised Friedman's efforts. "It must have been a tremendous satisfaction to you to find a system of constructing codes reducing the methods of compilation 75 percent over present methods," wrote the colonel. "It's damn good work and I hope it will result to your benefit."[249]

Still, their rapport remained frosty. Fabyan, for instance, refused to re-print one of Friedman's Riverbank papers, stating quite bluntly, "I don't want to obligate myself to do anything which may not fit into my game at a certain time." In a subsequent note, the millionaire declared, "It may be egotism on my part, but so long as I pay the fiddler, I am going to have the privilege of selecting a few of the tunes." Suggesting an on-going bitterness about Friedman's departure for Washington, Fabyan also complained, "If I cannot have your work without restrictions, I will have to do without it."[250]

The colonel, although no longer Friedman's boss, still tried to issue directives. In March 1921, for instance, he wrote about two conferences that would discuss a paper on a 13th century manuscript alleged to contain creative and, as yet, un-translated ciphers, and he told Friedman to "attend both of these meetings and give me a report on it."[251] In this instance, the code breaker acted as requested.

Friedman, meanwhile, kept asking the colonel to publish his non-government papers or to sponsor his independent research. Often the appeals were subtle, as in March 1921 when he suggested, "I only wish I had the resources necessary to carry out one or two of the projects I have in mind."[252] On other occasions, they negotiated tensely. When Fabyan wanted a letter deciphered and a short report written, Friedman demanded $150 upfront. The colonel responded with an offer of only $50, so Friedman huffily declared he would complete the assignment without a fee only if Fabyan would guarantee he was listed as the report's author. The colonel did not reply.

Chapter 8
WITHDRAWAL

A lifetime of chain smoking caught up with Fabyan in the early 1930's. The vibrant and athletic body slowly lost its spark. The gruff and opinionated motivator became increasingly quiet.

Health, however, wasn't the only factor in the colonel's decline. The Friedmans' departure deprived Fabyan of the camaraderie and tension he cherished, and it had depressed him to watch Mrs. Gallup's demise. Although the colonel relished Paul Sabine's efforts with motion pictures and sound stages, Riverbank's primary efforts on tuning forks and acoustic testing were not enough to inspire this "ideas man."

The dry-goods business, moreover, became more competitive and profits less certain. Bliss Fabyan & Company, in fact, was forced to reorganize in the early 1930's, an event that caused George and his brother Francis to back away from management activities.

The colonel's withdrawal from Riverbank responsibilities occurred fairly quickly as the new decade advanced. With lung cancer sapping his energy and enthusiasm, his inspection strolls through the estate became slower, and his visits to the laboratories became less frequent. His pranks, as well as his hell-chair lectures, ceased. Pain seemed to be his constant companion.

With no heir to inspire, Fabyan began to arrange for Riverbank's shrinkage. Wanting some physical legacy, he decided to donate most of the estate after Nelle's death in order to create a county park.

The 69-year-old colonel passed away at his villa on May 17, 1936. His Riverbank colleagues, as requested, stopped the lighthouse's flashing and they cut in half the chimes from the tower bell. Fabyan's body was taken to his family plot in Boston's Forest Hill Cemetery and placed beneath a simple headstone: "George Fabyan 1867 – 1936."

Riverbank After Fabyan

Nelle Fabyan and Belle Cumming for several years managed Riverbank's transition. Although not as showy, colorful, or committed to science as her husband, Nelle displayed particular skill at managing the estate's gardens and animals. Her livestock, bred in what she called the "scientific barn" south of the laboratories, featured several prize-winning creatures, including her favorite Jersey bull, named "Ocean Blue," which she showed at fairs all across the country. Nelle remained a proud member of the National Livestock Breeders Association and maintained a box seat for the annual shows at Chicago's amphitheater. She also raised homing pigeons and managed several kennels of English Bulldogs and German Shepherds.

Recalling her father's work as an Indian agent, Nelle also organized frequent presentations for her friends and neighbors on Native American culture. For several summers, she constructed, on the Fabyan Island in the middle of the Fox River, mock villages that revealed the customs of different tribes from the region.

Although a millionaire who enjoyed shopping regularly at the fashionable Marshall Field's department store in Chicago's Loop and who entertained regularly and lavishly at her villa, Nelle could be tight with her money. For instance, when a chauffeur took her to coffee or tea with her two sisters, both of whom lived near Riverbank, she regularly waited for them to pick up the check.

Still, Nelle was remembered for her kindness and graciousness, as someone who tempered her husband's rough edges. She died on July 22, 1939, at the age of 70, having struggled for a couple of years with her own cancer. After a service at the estate, she was buried with her husband in Boston.

Nelle's will called for the creation of a Fabyan Foundation, which subsequently sold some of Riverbank's non-productive assets, invested those funds, and made annual grants to improve education in Geneva. The fund has funneled almost $2 million into the city, including $1.2 million for the school district and $700,000 for the library.[253]

Belle Cumming for several years oversaw the foundation and continued to administer Riverbank, although activities – other than the testing and production of world-class tuning forks – languished without the colonel's fervent curiosity. Originally from Scotland, she finally visited her homeland after the colonel's death since he, when alive, had argued vigorously against her traveling overseas. Belle was killed in 1946 in a freak railroad accident. On the night of May 12, she had driven to the Geneva station in order for a friend to catch the late train back east into Chicago. They waited patiently at the crossing for a slow-moving east-bound freight to pass. No other west-bounds were expected at that hour, yet when Belle began to drive through the intersection, the delayed but fast-moving *Los Angeles Flyer* slammed the car. It's both sad and ironic that this woman who figuratively kept Riverbank's trains running on time was killed by a late running train.

The Fabyans' wills declared the estate – including the villa, island, gardens, and windmill – should be made available for the public's enjoyment. Although the colonel spent millions upgrading the property, Kane County in 1939 obtained the buildings and fields east of Route 31 for only $70,000. The structures west of the Lincoln Highway initially remained controlled by the Fabyan estate, but the Illinois Institute of Technology took over the laboratories in 1947, and they subsequently were purchased by a private corporation that upgraded the buildings in 2010 in order to produce electronic equipment. The firm making tuning forks, which kept the Riverbank name, moved to an office in downtown Geneva.

Beginning in the late 1970s, preservation groups, including Friends of Fabyan and Preservation Partners of the Fox Valley, began to refurbish the villa, which had been virtually abandoned for several years. Local volunteers raised funds to restore the verandas and, thereby, distinguish the house again as a Frank Lloyd Wright project. After extensive cleaning and reconstruction, the home reopened to the public in 1981. For an extended period, it served as a natural history museum, a favorite outing location for nearby schoolchildren. The living room featured Fabyan's carefully preserved buffalo family (including father, mother, and baby) and a cinnamon-colored bear rearing on its hind legs. In the corner stood a suit of armor made in the year 856 for the Japanese emperor Seiwa Genii. Several glass cases in the dining room displayed armadillos and other exotic creatures, as well as Nelle's collection of more than 400 Native-American artifacts, including locally-made arrowheads, skinning knives, a mortar and pestle, and hunting blades. Another case held an Egyptian "mummy," which researchers had debunked as a carnival exhibit and was probably a prize from Fabyan's collection of unclaimed freight. While the displays conveyed a sense of the colonel's eclectic interests, the non-profit preservation groups hope to progressively move many of them to other estate buildings in order to restore the villa to its condition when George and Nelle lived there.

The refurbished Fabyan windmill was placed on the National Register of Historic Places in 1979, and other preservation work focused on the gazebo, maid's house, and garage. Illinois officials converted the North Western rail line that had delivered Fabyan's "junk" into a popular bike and walking path along the Fox River.

Most of Riverbank's researchers moved on, and several enjoyed additional accomplishments. The Friedmans, for instance, debunked many of

WITHDRAWAL

the Bacon-is-Shakespeare theories, as well as cracked Japan's secret Purple ciphers during World War II. Paul Sabine, meanwhile, patented sound-absorbing doors and plasters, and he helped the U.S. military detect Japanese and German submarines.

Acoustics After Fabyan

Fabyan died as Hitler's troops invaded the Rhineland and Mussolini's forces conquered Ethiopia, but Paul Sabine continued the colonel's tradition of reaching out to the U.S. government when war threatened. Riverbank, Sabine offered, could help the Allies test acoustically the designs for ships, submarines, and airplanes. While his Geneva team performed some such work, Sabine moved temporarily to Harvard University's Underwater Sound Laboratory where he helped develop new means to detect enemy submarines. In October 1945, as World War II ended, he returned to Riverbank, developed more accurate tuning forks, and resumed testing various corporations' wallboard, cork, and wood siding.

Like his distant cousin, Paul Sabine worked several fronts simultaneously. He consulted on the construction or refurbishment of numerous buildings, including Boston's Federal Reserve Bank, Chicago's Civic Opera House, Philadelphia's Fels Planetarium, and the theaters of New York's Radio City. He patented a sound-insulating door, and he published several articles in *The American Architect* to explain how acoustical tiles, painted plasters, and other sound-capturing materials could cut down a room's reverberation and noise.

Colleagues described Paul Sabine as principled, loyal, and hard working. Although quite serious at the lab, he possessed a sharp but self-deprecating wit and obtained a reputation as a joker. When introduced at conferences as an acoustical expert, he would define such "as a man who could collect money from a person by telling him something he already knew in a language he doesn't understand."[254]

Yet when he served as a Geneva alderman debating zoning ordinances and snow removal policies, he displayed an aura of seriousness, justice, and

145

moral rightness. His fellow elected officials observed that the diligent politician "asks more questions than all the rest of us put together."

The son of a Methodist minister, Sabine was particularly interested in the connection between science and god, and he published two books on the subject. "When scientific and religious thinking go far enough," he wrote to a friend, "they discover that they both are facets of a single shaft of eternal truth."[255] He even discussed his views about the nature of man, god, and the physical world on Edward R. Murrow's radio show, "This I Believe."

Paul Sabine died in December 1958 and was buried in his beloved Geneva.

Bacon-Shakespeare After Fabyan

William Friedman never publicly attacked Fabyan when his benefactor was alive, but he and Elizabeth also never abandoned their skepticism of the colonel's Bacon-is-Shakespeare theories. Coming full circle at the end of their distinguished government careers, the Friedmans used their substantial cryptographic expertise to increasingly criticize what they considered the illogical arguments advanced by Fabyan and Gallup. Elizabeth assembled a vast collection of documents and papers associated with Baconian ciphers, and the code-breaking couple purchased a row house on Capitol Hill to be close to research facilities at the Library of Congress and Folger Shakespeare Library, which contained an extensive collection of First Folios.

William and Elizabeth spent three full years writing a 100,000-word manuscript, initially titled *The Cryptologist Looks at Shakespeare*. Part of their motivation was to understand the mindset of fervent Shakespearean skeptics. "Every case that I have examined presents clear-cut evidence of self-delusion of a very interesting character," wrote William. "It is amazing to see how wishful thinking can distort what might otherwise be fairly normal minds."[256]

The Friedmans felt Fabyan's interest resulted largely from his large ego and his craving for celebrity. "It was not far from his mind that if Bacon were proved to be Shakespeare," they wrote, "Mrs. Gallup would also be seen to be (administratively and financially) Colonel Fabyan, which would be very satisfactory."[257]

Yet William and Elizabeth didn't limit their criticism to the colonel. When Conrad Arensberg, the wealthy art collector, invited the Friedmans in the 1920's to direct a California-based Francis Bacon Foundation that he would subsidize to the tune of one million dollars, they welcomed the chance to study Bacon's writings and codes but they expressed no interest in trying to prove the Elizabethan scientist wrote Shakespeare's plays and poems. In fact, William mocked Arensberg's cryptographic approach, which he described as: "Take any initial letters you like, as long as you take them from consecutive words at the beginning or the end of any line, or from consecutive lines, or both. Rearrange the letters to form any word or phrase you care to choose, and serve with flourish." Friedman later wrote to a friend that Arensberg "was not at all impressed by my telling him that I had applied his method (of numerology) to random paragraphs of the *Los Angeles Times* and had found Baconian claims in them."[258]

William and Elizabeth expressed no "professional or emotional stake in any particular claim to the authorship of Shakespeare's plays," yet the Friedmans clearly scoffed at several of the theories. William, for instance, targeted the amateur cryptologists who "pointed out that in the 46th Psalm, the 46th word is 'Shake' and the 46th from the end of the Psalm is 'speare.'" With a mocking tone, he asked, "Isn't that quite adequate to prove Shakespeare was the author of the Bible – at least the King James version? Get out your copy and begin counting if you doubt this fact."[259]

The Friedmans portrayed themselves as scientists demanding translations be replicable by others. Any cryptanalyst's decipherment, they wrote, "must be unbiased, systematic, and logically sound. It must be free from appeals to insight, clear of guesswork, and should avoid imponderables like the plague; in a word, it must be scientific." Expanding on cryptography's tension between art and science, they stated: "There is an art in devising ciphers, and an art in breaking them down. But in setting out his results, a cryptologist is above all a man of science."[260]

GEORGE FABYAN

William and Elizebeth examined the theories of numerous anti-Stratfordians, including Natalie Rice Clark (who argued Bacon devised a compass clock dial that dictated the placement of various letters and words in the First Folios); Edward Johnson (who believed Bacon created a spatial pattern to hide secrets within the plays); William Stone Booth (who selected the initial letters of various words to "discover" an acrostic message or Francis Bacon's signature); and Wallace McCook Cunningham (a distinguished economist who argued Bacon and a group of Rosicrucians and Freemasons used Shakespeare's characters as foils for contemporary history.

The Friedmans systematically discounted each advocate as being sincere but misdirected. They wrote, "The worst that can be said of even the most bizarre of them is that they are in other respects sensible people who, in pursuing the elusive proofs they hope one day to discover, have allowed good judgment to be undermined."[261]

William and Elizebeth directed most of their attention to Mrs. Elizebeth Wells Gallup's cryptographic theories. "Of all the ciphers said to be present in the plays," they wrote, "the biliteral cipher is the most scientific, the most plausible, the most practical, and, because it was invented by Francis Bacon, the most appealing."[262] They also appreciated why Gallup would be curious about the different fonts within Shakespeare's First Folios, as well as why she would suspect the gifted Bacon hid ciphers within the printings of Elizabethan texts.

Yet the Friedmans argued Gallup's translations did not pass the basic tests of cryptography – that they be scientific, "clear of guesswork," and repeatable by other analysts. The differences within the Shakespeare folios between the "a-form" and "b-form," in fact, were so minute that different examiners could not agree on their assignments, let alone replicate the translations with identical results. Gallup's interpretations, concluded the Friedmans, were only "an exercise of personal judgment, which cannot be understood, communicated, checked, or duplicated."[263] Put another way, they stated Gallup simply found in the texts what she wanted to find. As

Elizebeth reflected, "I can state categorically that neither I nor any other one of the industrious research workers at Riverbank ever succeeded in extracting a single long sentence of a hidden message; nor did one of us so much as reproduce, independently, a single complete sentence which Mrs. Gallup had already deciphered and published."[264]

Fabyan, suspecting the unscientific nature of Gallup's classifications, had hired a professional typographer, F.W. Goudy, to examine the first editions of Bacon's work. William Friedman was aware of the consultant, but the colonel never released his report. So it was a surprise when Elizebeth discovered Goudy's findings in the summer of 1954 as she was scouring the Fabyan papers donated to the Library of Congress. The colonel and Mrs. Gallup, obviously, had not been pleased with the typographer's conclusions "that some of the variations in letter-forms were due to this makeshift of the printers, and some others simply due to the motley collection of fonts all used indiscriminately together." In essence, the colonel's own consultant had debunked the Bacon-is-Shakespeare theory.

William and Elizebeth hired their own consultant, an FBI document examiner referred to them by J. Edgar Hoover. That special agent's report, filled with drawings and diagrams, contained only four sentences, the most decisive of which read: "No characteristics were found which support the classification into two fonts, such as a-font and b-font." Based on the consultant's findings and their own analyses, the Friedmans concluded, "We can state quite firmly that the biliteral thesis in any strict sense is invalid; it is just not true that the printer used two and only two letter forms which can be identified a- and b-forms and deciphered."[265]

The Friedmans also questioned whether Gallup's theories passed the basic laugh test. "The serious and open-minded examiner of Baconian theories is forced to ask himself," the code breakers wrote, "how it can be asserted that one great genius wrote Bacon's works, and allegedly the Shakespeare plays, as mere vehicles for the fundamentally more important secret messages; yet the secret utterances, now at last deciphered, are poverty-stricken in intellectual content."

Gallup's deciphered messages, indeed, were surprisingly devoid of the grace and logic befitting a gifted writer. From the prologue to Shakespeare's *Troilus and Cressida*, Mrs. Gallup "translated" only this convoluted claim from Sir Francis Bacon:

> *Francis St. Alban, descended from the mighty heroes of Troy, loving and revering these noble ancestors, hid in his writings Homer's Iliads and Odyssey (in cipher), with the Aeneid of the noble Virgil, prince of Latin poets, inscribing the letters to Elizabeth, R.*

Despite such criticisms of Baconians, the Friedmans acknowledged Sir Francis to be a genius who made substantial contributions to cryptography. William went so far as to credit Bacon's biliteral cipher with being the foundation for our digital age's use of zeros and ones: "Bacon was, in fact, the inventor of the binary code that forms the basis of modern … computers."[266]

As the Friedmans were editing their book, William suffered another psychiatric setback and spent several months at Mt. Alto Hospital and George Washington University Hospital. When he finally returned to the project, the couple rushed an application for the Folger Shakespeare Award, which their manuscript won in April 1955.

Cambridge University Press agreed to publish the book, but editors demanded major cuts and renamed it *The Shakespearean Ciphers Examined*. Although happy to have the publication released in October 1957, the Friedmans disliked the new title because it suggested ciphers actually existed within the Bard's writings, a theory their manuscript repudiated.

Cryptography After Fabyan

As Germany again began to threaten her neighbors, the U.S. government again drafted Elizebeth for a sensitive assignment – establishing cryptographic systems for what was to become the Office of Strategic Services. She worked closely with General William Donovan to develop secure codes and ciphers for the Americans and to break those deployed by the Nazis.

William, meanwhile, focused on Purple, the cipher used by Japan's Foreign Office beginning in late 1938 to communicate with its embassies around the world. Considered to be the most complex cryptographic structure to date, Purple (or *Angoki Taipu B*, as it was known to the Japanese) replaced ciphers Tokyo knew the Americans were reading. With the new system's introduction, the U.S. lost its intelligence pipeline.

Packed within the third floor of the giant Munitions Building on Washington, D.C.'s National Mall, William and the Signal Intelligence Service (SIS) obtained regular intercepts from U.S. listening posts around the world, but they made little progress deciphering the new Japanese messages. Adding to their frustration were Washington's steamy summer, constant construction noise, and a fire that left the offices smoky and drenched.

As the SIS staff grew to almost 300 and moved to Arlington Hall across the Potomac River in Virginia, Friedman climbed the bureaucratic ladder but spent less and less time tackling Purple. His management assignment changed in February 1939, however, when General Joseph Mauborgne directed him to drop all other activities and pursue the military's top priority of cracking the Japanese code. (During the same period in Britian, Alan Turing, a brilliant Cambridge fellow and intellectual father of the computer, faced similar pressures to solve Germany's Enigma messages.)

Friedman became obsessed by the assignment, rising in the middle of nights, going downstairs to drink coffee, eat sandwiches, and pace throughout his house. The grueling routine continued for month after month, while in Europe German tanks rolled across Poland and Hitler's planes bombed Norway, Netherlands, France, and southern England. Friedman's insomnia and stress eventually led to a nervous breakdown, and he entered Walter Reed Hospital's psychiatric ward on January 4, 1941, diagnosed with extreme fatigue "due to prolonged overwork on a top secret project."

When he returned to the office several months later, some colleagues said he seemed in control, yet close friends worried about his nagging depression. One recalled Friedman placing a long rope in the back seat of his car and declaring: "I'm looking for a tree to hang myself."[267]

Also delaying the deciphering process were the lack of trusted Japanese translators and the slow delivery of intercepted messages. Those captured by Hawaii's listening station, for instance, were packaged together once a week and sent to Washington by a commercial airliner. When bad weather restricted flights, the packages moved more slowly by ship.

Cipher traffic increased in early September 1940 when Japanese, German, and Italian officials started to prepare for the Berlin signing of the Tripartite Pact that pledged cooperation among these Axis countries. Communications rose particularly between Tokyo and Japan's ambassador to Germany, Baron Oshima, who had gained the trust of Joachim von Ribbentrop, the German foreign minister. Finally having more material to examine, Friedman slowly began to translate portions of Oshima's detailed reports about Hitler's plans and pending operations.

A few Japanese officials suspected Purple had been compromised. The foreign minister, in fact, warned his ambassador in Washington, "According to a fairly reliable source of information it appears almost certain that the United States Government is reading your code messages. Please let me know whether you have any suspicions of the above." Yet the Japanese ambassador did what bureaucrats often do – he formed an investigative committee and concluded the problem was not his. With such assurances, Tokyo continued to believe Purple was secure.

Yet by late September, Friedman's team had devised a deciphering contraption with hundreds of multicolored wires and switches. Without ever having seen the Japanese cipher machine, they constructed a clone that offered ungarbled texts of Tokyo's secret messages.

Those texts increasingly revealed Japan's rising anger toward the United States. One deciphered message asked Baron Oshima to meet with Hitler in Berlin in order to explain "the extreme danger that war may suddenly break out between the Anglo-Saxon nations and Japan through some clash of arms." Such a conflict, the memo warned, could "come more quickly than anyone dreams."[268]

Not long after, Friedman translated messages instructing Japanese ambassadors around the globe to destroy their code and cipher machines.

War seemed imminent, but the Americans could obtain no specifics about the time or place of Tokyo's first attack.

The U.S. Navy's listening station on Bainbridge Island in Washington's Puget Sound intercepted several messages early in the morning on Sunday, December 7, 1941. The 14-page rambling translation began with Tokyo's response to the recent American demand that it withdraw from China in return for the United States restoring trade and returning Japanese funds. But the latter pages declared Japan's decision to break off negotiations, and it ordered its ambassador in Washington to "please submit to the United States Government (if possible to the Secretary of State) our reply to the United States at 1:00 pm on the 7th, your time."

Friedman's SIS colleagues deciphered that message at about 9:00 am, which was 3:00 am in Hawaii. The Washington-based duty officer frantically tried to locate senior officials, including General George Marshall, the Army Chief of Staff, but he had gone horseback riding. When told of an urgent message upon his return at about 9:45 am, Marshall decided to drive to his Washington office, where he carefully and slowly read the entire 14 pages, ignoring the duty officer's plea that he skip to the end and its declaration of a 1:00 pm deadline.

Finally alarmed by the text's ominous warning, Marshall decided to avoid the "scrambler" that did not offer a secure telephone connection to General Walter Scott in Hawaii. Instead, he sent an urgent warning through the War Department's Message Center. Unfortunately, the receiving station at Fort Shafter in Hawaii wasn't operating, so the message finally appeared at RCA's Honolulu office at 7:33 am, where it was put into an envelope for delivery to the commanding general. Japanese bombs began to fall on Ford Island in Pearl Harbor at 7:55 am.

Friedman was working at home that Sunday morning. When he heard the news reports, according to Elizabeth, he despondently paced back and forth, muttering, "But they knew, they knew, they knew."

In fact, they didn't know. Friedman later admitted the surprise associated with Pearl Harbor's bombing resulted from a "series of accidents that contrived together to prevent due warning." Several years after the conflict, he expounded further in response to a question about the revisionist theory that U.S. government officials intentionally allowed the bombing to occur in order to provoke public support for a war. "There were no messages which can be said to have disclosed exactly where and when the attack would be made," Friedman wrote. "Hence I do not see how President Roosevelt could have avoided the attack by advance knowledge from reading such messages. In my opinion only certain members of what may be called the Extreme Right Wing believe this fable. No reliable and reputable historians believe it."[269]

Friedman subsequently remained a key member of the Operation Magic teams that decoded Japanese ciphers. Particularly valuable were his translations of Baron Oshima's transcripts that allowed General Dwight Eisenhower to better plan D-Day. According to William Crowell, deputy director in the early 1990's of the National Security Agency, Hitler before the invasion gave Oshima a guided tour of Normandy. As a result, the Baron knew the "number of (German) troops and where every gun was placed and it was all in the (deciphered) message. Normandy wouldn't have happened … it may have been some other beach and it wouldn't have been as successful if there hadn't been that intercept."[270]

Friedman's team in mid 1942 also decoded Japan's attack plan for the Battle of Midway, allowing Admiral Chester Nimitz to preempt Tokyo's strategy and fight off a superior force, halting Japan's offensive in the Pacific. Tokyo's texts subsequently became increasingly despondent, demonstrating a growing reluctance to fight further. It's well known that President Harry Truman, while attending the Potsdam conference that settled the European war, received confirmation of a successful nuclear bomb test at Alamagordo, New Mexico. Less well known is his briefing packet also contained translations of Japanese messages describing the need for surrender and peace. Several years after Truman made his decision to deploy atomic weapons on Hiroshima and Nagasaki, Friedman wrote, "If only I had a channel of communication to the President I would have recommended that he not drop the bomb – since the war would be over within a week."[271]

An unexpected outcome of breaking Purple was discovery of the Soviet Union's extensive espionage within the United States and England during World War II and the early days of the Cold War. After breaking messages between the Japanese and Finns that revealed Moscow's codes, Friedman and his colleagues eventually deciphered 2,900 Russian transcripts that verified the spying of Julius Rosenberg, Alger Hiss, Harry Dexter White, Kim Philby, Donald Maclean, and almost 200 other American and British officials.

This story began not long after the signing of the 1939 Nazi-Soviet Pact of Non-Aggression when U.S. Army intelligence officers started to accumulate Russia's encoded messages. For five years they made no effort at decipherment, believing Russia to be an ally and considering it bad form to read a friend's mail. Yet beginning in 1944, in order to understand the Soviet military's capabilities and Stalin's objectives, the U.S. Army's Signal Intelligence Service (SIS) established a program, code named Venona, to translate messages from the Soviet Union's intelligence agencies. At the time, no one imagined the ciphers would reveal an extensive espionage network within Washington's agencies and America's industry.

Moscow's cryptosystem should have been unbreakable. According to the NSA's William Crowell, it first "consisted of a code book in which letters, words, and phrases were equated to numbers." Translating those numbers without the code book would itself have been a significant challenge, but the Soviets further complicated their system – creating a double encryption – by using a one-time pad that randomized the code.

The key to America's eventual success, said Crowell, "was that mistakes were made in the construction and use of the one-time pads – a fact that was discovered only through brute force and analysis of the message traffic."[272] It seems some Soviet official inadvertently reused pages from

GEORGE FABYAN

some of the one-time pads, but even with that discovery, it took SIS more than two years to obtain its first break into the KGB encryption. Still, the Americans translated only a fraction of the thousands of intercepted messages, and, unlike Japan's Purple code, none of Moscow's communications were read in real time.

The SIS's first real break came in late December 1946 when Meredith Gardner (from the University of Akron's language department) and Richard Hallock (from the University of Chicago's archeology department) – both of whom Friedman had recruited – discovered the encoded messages periodically repeated numbers. Working with primitive computers that used punch cards and vacuum tubes, they and others painstakingly deciphered messages sent in 1944 from Moscow to its New York office that revealed Soviet espionage within the Manhattan Project's atomic bomb operations at Los Alamos National Laboratory.

Translations were spotty. The best record occurred with the Moscow-to-New York messages from 1944, when 49 percent of the interceptions were eventually translated. With 1943 traffic, however, the percentage reached only 15 percent, and for 1942 just 2 percent were readable. The Moscow-to-Washington messages were even more difficult to decipher, with just 1.5 percent of the 1944 communications translated. Overall, the National Security Agency estimated the Soviets encoded two million messages, of which SIS decoded in part or fully only 2,900.

The translations, however, revealed startling and frightening information about Soviet spies working within the Departments of State and Treasury, Office of Strategic Service, and even Arlington Hall and the White House. Although each spy had a code name, which sometimes changed, it became clear America's atomic secrets were being provided to the Russians by Klaus Fuchs, Alan Nun May, and Donald Maclean, a member of the Cambridge Five spy ring. According to two historians, the Venona transcripts revealed the existence of 349 well-placed Americans working as Soviet spies, yet less than half could be identified by their real names.[273]

Harry Truman learned of the secret Soviet messages about a month after he entered the White House but he expressed skepticism of the translations, saying the early decipherment effort sounded "like a fairy story." Yet the new president increasingly feared the House Un-American Activities Committee, an ardent critic of the New Deal, would use the revelations to blast Democrats for allowing communists to work within the government.

The Soviets learned of the U.S. project in the late 1940's, in part because they had planted a KGB agent, named Bill Weisband, within Arlington Hall, and in part because Kim Philby, a British diplomat assigned to liaison with American cryptanalysts, regularly passed on summaries of Venona's translations to his Soviet handlers. Although Moscow officials could do little about Washington's efforts and certainly couldn't take back their messages, they did warn some of their agents and brought others back to Russia before their identities could be revealed.

The FBI decided against using Venona transcripts during the legal prosecutions of Soviet spies, largely for fear of exposing the government's cryptography capabilities. An agency memo also noted "the fragmentary nature of the messages and the extensive use of cover names therein make positive identification of the subjects difficult."[274]

The Venona deciphers, however, strengthened the spying charges against Julius Rosenberg, even as they suggested his wife Ethel was engaged only as an accomplice. Rosenberg's trading of atomic secrets was not as damaging as first thought, yet Venona revealed he did pass on to Moscow thousands of classified pages from Emerson Radio as well as design and production reports on Lockheed's P-80 jet fighter.

The Venona files showed – according to Senator Daniel Patrick Moynihan, who chaired a congressional investigation after the transcripts were released – that Alger Hiss, while a State Department and United Nations official, was a Russian spy. Said the senator, "Hiss was indeed a Soviet agent and appears to have been regarded by Moscow as its most important."[275]

GEORGE FABYAN

The translated messages also allowed Army, FBI, and CIA officials to better understand KGB operations. They learned how Moscow arranged security for its secret meetings with agents, its countermeasures against American surveillance, its detection of U.S. bugging devices, and its practices to ensure the loyalty of U.S.-based Soviet personnel. One set of messages described how the KGB tracked down Soviet sailors who had deserted from merchant ships in San Francisco and other U.S. ports. Others detailed how the Russian-based agency assessed and recruited American communists for espionage work.

After World War II, Friedman accepted a series of high-level assignments. At the newly formed Army Security Agency, he directed communications research. At its successor, the Armed Forces Security Agency, he served as cryptologic consultant. And finally at the newly integrated National Security Agency (NSA), he became special assistant to the director.

Friedman also received impressive awards and praise. The War Department in 1944 identified him as one of the first recipients of its highest honor, the Commendation for Exceptional Civilian Service. Two years later, he obtained the Medal for Merit, considered to be the civilian equivalent of the military's Distinguished Service Medal, with recognition for "outstanding service conspicuously above the usual." He was presented in 1955 with the National Security Medal, joining J. Edgar Hoover as the only person with both that award and the Medal for Merit. *Smithsonian Magazine* hailed him as "the greatest maker and breaker of secret messages in history – the Harry Houdini of codes and ciphers."[276]

Despite such accolades, Friedman became increasingly agitated about his profession. He had advocated for a centralized agency to gather and decipher intelligence, yet he felt the NSA was becoming a wasteful bureaucracy more interested in fancy computers than the art of cryptanalysis. He also lamented the National Security Agency's abuse of its growing capacity to tap telephones and bug electronic equipment, as well as its imposition of excessive secrecy, even reclassifying several of Friedman's own papers that had been in public libraries for years. "I am hampered by restrictions," he complained to a friend, "which are at these times so intolerable and nonsensical that it is a wonder that I have been able to retain my sanity."[277]

Unfortunately, Friedman was losing his grip on that sanity. He entered Mt. Alto Hospital in December 1949, complaining of profound depression. Hating the psychotic unit, he transferred in March 1950 to the George Washington University Hospital, where he received six electroshock treatments and was discharged a month later. According to his psychiatrist, "Although he had entered the hospital in a very glum, morose, deeply depressed, and potentially suicidal mood, he was almost elated when he was discharged, and in a characteristically effusive way he kissed the nurses goodbye in a rather avuncular fashion."[278]

The Friedmans, as explained above, spent substantial time after government service writing a book challenging Fabyan's and Gallup's claims that Sir Francis Bacon authored Shakespeare's plays. Elizabeth periodically consulted with the Coast Guard and Treasury Department on codes, and she created a secure communications system for the International Monetary Fund. William, moreover, was called upon three times for sensitive government missions to smooth over tensions with British colleagues who more and more distrusted America's growing spy operations.

Yet William's relations with the NSA became increasingly tense. In late December 1958, three agents confiscated from Friedman's home 48 items of his cryptographic collection, including an original copy of his own *The Index of Coincidence*. "The secrecy virus reached its height of virulence," he griped, "and the NSA took away from me everything that some nitwit regarded as being of a classified nature." Although the agency never took away his security clearance, the increasingly paranoid Friedman periodically hired outside consultants to ensure the NSA had not bugged his house.

Depression returned. A note from the early 1960's read: "Feeling of being 'has-been' unendurable. (I'm) jealous of men who have been able to retire and go to other jobs of usefulness and carry on, but not I."[279]

Part of Friedman's depression related to his growing concerns about the morality of cryptographic work and the National Security Agency's pervasive and invasive spying. Sometimes lamenting his early decision to abandon genetics for cryptography, he complained about the fine line between the benefits of breaking the codes of enemies and the dangers of invading the privacy of American citizens. "My own feelings on the ethical point at issue are quite ambivalent – and have been for a long time," he wrote. "I have often wondered whether a good portion of my psychic difficulties over the years are not attributable, in part at least, to that ambivalence."[280]

Friedman returned to a hospital psychiatric unit in February 1963, and his doctor found he had no desire "to go on." According to a friend: "He felt that he had been grossly hurt by the people at NSA because they distrusted him and deliberately reclassified all his papers so that he would not be able to sell any of the historical ones, and he began feeling that the people at NSA were 'out to get him.'"[281]

After a series of heart attacks, Friedman died on November 3, 1969. Elizabeth lived another 11 years, during which time she assembled and sold the couple's unclassified papers to the George C. Marshall Foundation at the Virginia Military Institute. William was buried with full military honors at Arlington National Cemetery, where the epitaph on his tomb reads the Baconian axiom: "Knowledge is Power." The NSA renamed the main hall at its Fort Meade headquarters the "William F. Friedman Memorial Auditorium."

Chapter 9
LEGACY

Successful businessmen often display substantial egos. With larger-than-life personalities, some retire and underwrite universities and museums (John Rockefeller and Paul Mellon). Some gain almost celebrity status and become known for their investment and business tips (Berkshire Hathaway's Warren Buffett or General Electric's Jack Welch), racing yachts (Oracle's Larry Ellison), or charitable contributions (Microsoft's Bill Gates).

George Fabyan's own ego certainly was sizeable, enlarged as it was by his uncanny ability to make money and to achieve success in the disparate fields of business, science, and military/international affairs. Yet the colonel was unique among tycoons. When he had accumulated "enough," he sought fulfillment from research that would improve humanity's lot. He wrote no books, offered few tips, and gave away little of his money to independent charities. Fabyan viewed himself as "mankind's servant – for the fun of it,"[282] and he displayed rather eccentric fancies and idiosyncrasies.

Reflecting his era's growing interest in science and its faith in progress, the colonel's pervasive curiosity sparked substantial achievements in acoustics, cryptography, and genetics. Before governments and foundations provided such support, Fabyan sponsored research for its own sake,

GEORGE FABYAN

creating a model for independent research centers. No doubt his levitation machine and Shakespearean claims were, at best, odd, yet he supported and motivated researchers who, among other things, helped end a world war, enable wireless transmissions, write and break ciphers, improve auditoriums, allow the deaf to hear, and synchronize electricity generation. An Illinois newspaper observed that "no problem of mankind was beneath his notice."[283]

The colonel accepted numerous awards from the Japanese, French, and United States governments, and he enjoyed regaling reporters about the wonders of Riverbank's investigations. Still, he did relatively little to advance his own image. He authored no autobiography, hired no public relations specialist, and made no major contributions to high-profile institutions that might name buildings after him.

Instead, Fabyan inspired a diverse and rather independent and temperamental group of thinkers, several of whom became respected leaders in their fields. Their scientific explorations produced significant success but also provoked a great deal of individual stress, so it's perhaps no coincidence that two of the colonel's best known colleagues suffered mentally. Wallace Sabine, frustrated at failing to live up to his own perfectionism, burned his papers in Harvard Yard. William Friedman, exhausted by work and frustrated by being a Jew in the WASPy world of federal government bureaucracy, spent months in and out of institutions. It is a testament to Fabyan's managerial and motivational skills that Friedman, despite having numerous reasons to distrust (and even despise) the colonel, maintained cordial and working relations with his previous boss and benefactor.

Fabyan displayed numerous contradictions. He could be humorous and generous as well as brash, crass, and domineering. He was born a Boston Brahmin, but he dressed down and often reverted to childish pranks. He mingled with presidents, Hollywood stars, and elite scientists, yet he savored collecting junk at railroad yards. He dropped out of high school, but he displayed wide-ranging intellectual curiosity. He was conservative, fiercely patriotic, and supportive of the military establishment, yet his private life could verge on the scandalous. He enjoyed the spotlight and entertained celebrities, but he moved the country toward increased secrecy.

Despite such disparities, Fabyan's legacy persists on several levels. His estate – complete with gardens, windmill, and lighthouse – remains one of the most popular retreats in Chicago's western suburbs. The colonel's work, moreover, lives on at the National Security Agency, architectural firms, and medical research centers, and he and his investigators supplied the foundations on which cryptographers, designers, and scientists continue to build.

ACKNOWLEDGEMENTS

Writing is a solitary exercise, yet numerous people assisted this book's development.

Darlene Larson, a founder and leader of Friends of Fabyan, generously provided her insights and files. She and her group have done impressive work revealing the Fabyan record.

Lynn Dransoff, director of the Fabyan Villa Museum and Japanese Garden for the Preservation Partners of the Fox Valley, offered wonderful stories and pictures, as well as clarified facts. She and her colleagues organize informative public tours and have helped restore several of the estate's structures.

Ron Rawson at the Geneva History Center was extremely kind with his time and knowledge. His is one of the most impressive local libraries.

Paul Barron and Jeffrey Kozak manage the Research Library at the George C. Marshall Foundation. Located on the campus of the Virginia Military Institute (VMI), it houses the papers of William and Elizebeth Friedman. Both gentlemen welcomed me to their extensive collection and charming community.

Rose Mary Sheldon, a VMI history professor, compiled a wonderfully useful catalog of the Friedman papers. Colonel Sheldon also kindly answered my many questions and provided me with new materials and resources.

Leona Schecter, my literary agent, continued her persistent championship of my writing projects. Her dedication over the years is much appreciated.

Kathryn Tandy, most importantly, provided constant encouragement, sage suggestions, as well as beautiful pictures of Riverbank. I look forward to our continued collaborations.

ABOUT THE AUTHOR

Richard Munson is the author of several books. *Edison to Enron* recounts the history of electricity and proposes an innovation-based vision for the power industry. *The Cardinals of Capitol Hill* traces the machinations of congressional appropriators who control government spending, and *Cousteau: The Captain and His World* is a biography of the famed ocean explorer and filmmaker. Dick's articles on energy and environmental policy have appeared in numerous newspapers and journals.

Munson is senior vice president of Recycled Energy Development, a Chicago-based firm that finances, builds, and operates efficient cogeneration and clean waste-energy-recovery projects. Prior to joining RED, Dick directed the Northeast-Midwest Institute and coordinated with the Northeast-Midwest House and Senate Coalitions, which are bipartisan congressional caucuses that conduct policy research and draft legislation on agriculture, economic development, energy, environment, and manufacturing issues.

Munson also has served as director of the Solar Lobby and Center for Renewable Resources, co-coordinator of Sun Day, coordinator of the Environmental Action Foundation, and lecturer in history at the University of Michigan. He now sits on the boards of directors for the Center for Neighborhood Technology, Greenleaf Advisors, Institute for Health Policy Solutions, and Business Council for Sustainable Energy. He has received outstanding service awards from the Great Lakes Commission, U.S. Clean Heat and Power Association, and American Small Manufacturers Coalition.

ENDNOTES

1   "Col. Fabyan Dies, Science Patron," *Chicago Herald*, May 19, 1936.

2   Quote by Phyllis Fletcher (Reid), a Riverbank employee, from John W. Kopec, *The Sabines at Riverbank* (Los Altos, CA: Peninsula Publishing, 1997).

3   Quote by Elizebeth Friedman from James R. Chiles, "Breaking codes was this couple's lifetime career," *Smithsonian,* June 1987.

4   Bert Eisenhour, "A Collection of Memories From My Quarter-Century Association with the Riverbank Laboratories Department of Engineering," November 8, 2009.

5   "Col. Fabyan Dies, Science Patron," *Chicago Herald*, May 18, 1936.

6   Austin C. Lescarboura, "A Small Private Laboratory," *Scientific American*, September 1923.

7   Fabyan, George, *What I Know About the Future of Cotton and Domestic Goods*, (Chicago: Marshall-Jackson, Co., 1900).

8   Darlene Larson and Laura Hiebert, "The Fabyan Legacy," within *Geneva, Illinois: A History of Its Times and Places* (Geneva: Geneva Public Library District, 1977).

9   Elizebeth Friedman quoted in John W. Kopec, *The Sabines at Riverbank* (Los Altos, CA: Peninsula Publishing, 1997).

10   Quote by Phyllis Fletcher (Reid), within Kopec, *The Sabines at Riverbank*.

11   John W. Kopec, *The Sabines at Riverbank*. (Los Altos, CA: Peninsula Publishing, 1997).

12   Elizebeth Friedman as quoted in *Smithsonian*.

13 *Chicago Daily News*, April 22, 1921.

14 Amber Hare, "Fabyan's Riverbank Laboratories: where National Security smells as sweet," www.examiner.com, November 22, 2010.

15 *Chicago Daily Tribune*, "Army Conquers the Fox River Valley and Captures Recruits," July 19, 1917.

16 *Chicago Herald*, July 19, 1917.

17 Sammi King, "Col. Fabyan still remains memorable, interesting," *Daily Herald*, September 6, 2001.

18 Ibid..

19 Amber Hare, "Fabyan's Riverbank Laboratories: where National Security smells as sweet," examiner.com, November 14, 2010.

20 Ronald Clark, *The Man Who Broke Purple* (Boston: Little, Brown and Company, 1977)

21 *Chicago Herald*, July 12, 1915

22 Fabyan letter to Friedman, August 12, 1915. Friedman Collection, George C. Marshall Foundation, Lexington, Virginia.

23 Clark

24 Fabyan letter to Friedman, April 13, 1921.

25 Fabyan letter to Friedman, July 1, 1915.

26 Fabyan letter to Friedman, August 10, 1915.

27 *Chicago Daily News*, April 22, 1921.

28 Ibid.

29 *Chicago Herald*, July 12, 1915.

30 "History Behind Fabyan Preserve," *Aurora Beacon-News*, June 12, 1954.

31 John W. Kopec *The Sabines at Riverbank* (Los Altos, CA: Peninsula Publishing, 1997).

ENDNOTES

32 *Geneva Republican*, July 22, 1914.

33 Ibid.

34 *Geneva Republic*, June 20, 1914.

35 *Genealogical and Family History of the State of Maine*, Volume 4, by Henry Sweetser Burrage and Albert Roscoe Stubbs.

36 http://www.usgennet.org/family/bliss/bios/ma/cornel.htm

37 Joseph Henry Sawyer, *A History of Williston Seminary* (Easthampton, MA: The Trustees, 1917).

38 *Fabyan Images* (the periodic journal of Friends of Fabyan), Spring/Summer 1999.

39 Donald L. Miller, *City of the Century: The Epic of Chicago and the Making of America* (New York: Simon and Schuster, 1996).

40 Frank J. Piehl, "Chicago's Early Fight to 'Save Our Lake,'" *Chicago History* (Winter 1976-1977).

41 Lincoln Steffens, "The Shame of the Cities," *McClure's Magazine*, 1904.

42 Jon C. Teaford, *The Twentieth-Century American City* (Baltimore: Johns Hopkins University Press, 1993).

43 Quote in James R. Grossman, "African-American Migration to Chicago," in Melvin Holli and Peter d'A. Jones eds. *Ethnic Chicago: A Multicultural Portrait* (Grand Rapids, Michigan: Eerdmans Publishing Company, 1994)

44 Michael E. Parrish, *Anxious Decades: America in Prosperity and Depression, 1920-1941* (New York: W.W. Norton, 1992).

45 Robert G. Spinney, *City of Big Shoulders* (DeKalb, Illinois: Northern Illinois University Press, 2000).

46 George W. Norris, *Fighting Liberal: The Autobiography of George W. Norris* (N.Y.: Macmillan, 1945).

47 Frederick Lewis Allen, *Only Yesterday* (N.Y.: Harper & Row, 1931).

48 M.L. Ramsay, *Pyramids of Power: The Story of Roosevelt, Insull, and the Utility Wars* (N.Y.: Bobbs-Merrill, 1937).

49 Robert G. Spinney, *City of Big Shoulders* (DeKalb, Illinois: Northern Illinois University Press, 2000).

50 Dominic A. Pacyga, *Chicago: A Biography*.

51 Jay Robert Nash, *Makers and Breakers of Chicago from Long John Wentworth to Richard J. Daley* (Chicago: Academy Chicago Publishers, 1985).

52 Paul M. Green, "Anton J. Cermak: The Man and His Machine," in Paul M. Green and Melvin G. Holli, *The Mayors: The Chicago Political Tradition* (Carbondale, Illinois: Southern Illinois University Press, 1995).

53 Robert G. Spinney, *City of Big Shoulders* (DeKalb, Illinois: Northern Illinois University Press, 2000).

54 Ibid.

55 Dominic A. Pacyga, *Chicago: A Biography* (Chicago: University of Chicago Press, 2009). p 262

56 *Chicago Daily News*, April 22, 1921.

57 Ibid.

58 "Lab work labor of love for Mr. Riverbank," *The Beacon-News*.

59 Ann Pierotti, "Garden of Eden," *Geneva Chronicle*.

60 Kopec, *The Sabines at Riverbank*.

61 Kopec

62 Mable Elsworth Todd, "The Thinking Body: A Study of the Balancing Forces of Dynamic Man," (1937).

63 Austin C. Lescarboura, "A Small Private Laboratory," *Scientific American*, September 1923.

64 Author's interview with Richard Schlindwein, November 8, 2009.

ENDNOTES

65 Amber Hare, "Fabyan's Riverbank Laboratories: where National Security smells as sweet," examiner.com, November 22, 2010.

66 Richard F. Weingroff, "The Lincoln Highway," Office of Infrastructure, U.S. Department of Transportation, Federal Highway Administration, May 7, 2005.

67 Quote by John Thorpe in "George and Nelle Fabyan's Country Home," *Frank Lloyd Wright Quarterly*, Winter 1995.

68 Ibid.

69 Quote by John Thorpe in "George and Nelle Fabyan's Country Home," *Frank Lloyd Wright Quarterly*, Winter 1995.

70 Laura Franz Hiebert, "The Story Behind the Remarkable Fabyan Estate," June 1967.

71 Kopec.

72 *Geneva Republic*, August 12, 1914.

73 "The Country Estate in Illinois," *Historic Illinois*, February 1988.

74 Ibid.

75 Ibid.

76 "Fox River Goes on a Rampage," *Geneva Republican*, 22 January 1916.

77 *Chicago Daily News*, April 22, 1921.

78 Katherine Seigenthaler, "Out of Success Came Legends of Col. Fabyan," *Chicago Tribune*, August 10, 1987.

79 Ibid.

80 *Geneva Chronicle*, September 26, 1984.

81 Kane County Forest Preserve District, "Fabyan Windmill."

82 Russell Freeburg, "A Sound Idea Still Vibrates in Geneva Lab." *Chicago Sunday Tribune*, September 2, 1951.

83 Kane County Forest Preserve District, "The Fabyan Windmill: Self-Guided Tour Brochure."

84 Darlene Larson and Laura Hiebert, "The Fabyan Legacy."

85 Paul Sabine, "Historical Account of the Riverbank Laboratories," six-page undated report.

86 Norman Klein, "Fabyan Seeks to End Din of City Noises," *New York Times*, April 23, 1921.

87 Darlene Larson and Laura Hiebert, *The Fabyan Legacy*.

88 Wallace Clement Sabine, *Collected Papers on Acoustics* (New York: Dover Publications, 1964).

89 William Dana Orcutt, *Wallace Clement Sabine: A Study in Achievement* (Norwood, MA: Plimpton Press, 1933).

90 Letter from Charles McKim to Henry Lee Higginson, February 27, 1899. Henry Lee Higginson Collection, Baker Library, Harvard Business School.

91 Philip Hale, "First Symphony," *Boston Sunday Journal*, October 21, 1900.

92 "Boston's New Music-Hall," *New York Evening Post*, October 16, 1900.

93 "Music in Boston," *Musical Courier*, October 24, 1900.

94 W.C. Sabine, "Architectural Acoustics," *American Architect and Building News*, November 1898.

95 Richard Sennett, *The Fall of Public Man: On the Social Psychology of Capitalism* (New York: Alfred A. Knopf, 1977)

96 "Symphony Hall's Inaugural," *Boston Evening Transcript*, October 16, 1900.

97 Emily Thompson, *The Soundscape of Modernity*.

98 *True American and Commercial Advertiser* (October 31, 1807), quoted in John C. Van Horne, ed., *The Correspondence and Miscellaneous Papers*

ENDNOTES

of Benjamin Henry Latrobe, Vol. 2 (New Haven: Yale University Press, 1986).

99 Emily Thompson, *The Soundscape of Modernity* (Cambridge: The MIT Press, 2002).

100 Thompson, *The Soundscape of Modernity*.

101 Robert Twombley, *Louis Sullivan: His Life and Work* (Chicago: University of Chicago Press, 1986).

102 Thompson, *The Soundscape of Modernity*.

103 Wallace Clement Sabine, *Collected Papers on Acoustics* (New York: Dover Publications, 1964).

104 Sabine, *Collected Papers on Acoustics*.

105 Ibid.

106 Sabine, *Collected Papers on Acoustics*.

107 Ibid.

108 Emily Thompson, *The Soundscape of Modernity*.

109 Ibid.

110 Wallace Sabine, "Manufacture and Distribution of Acoustical Materials over the Past 25 Years," *Journal of the Acoustical Society of America (JASA)* (September 26, 1954).

111 James Loudon, "A Century of Progress in Acoustics," *Science* (December 27, 1901).

112 Letter from William Mead to Wallace Sabine, April 14, 1903. Quoted in Leland Roth, *McKim, Mead and White, Architects* (New York: Harper and Row, 1983).

113 Letter from Wallace Sabine to W.L. Krider, United States Gypsum Co., April 3, 1915.

114 William Dana Orcutt, *Wallace Clement Sabine: A Study in Achievement* (Norwood, MA: Plimpton Press, 1933).

115 From an introduction by Harvard Professor Frederick Hunt within Wallace Clement Sabine, *Collected Papers on Acoustics* (New York: Dover Publications, 1964).

116 Kopec, page 11

117 Theodore Lyman in preface to *Collected Papers on Acoustics – Wallace Clement Sabine (*Harvard University Press, 1922, vii)

118 Kopec, *The Sabines at Riverbank* (Los Altos, CA: Peninsula Publishing, 1997), page 62

119 *The American Architect*, July 2, 1919, "The Life Work of the Late Wallace C. Sabine, An Appreciation," by Paul E. Sabine.

120 Kopec, page 13

121 *The American Architect*, op cit

122 Paul Sabine, "The Beginnings in Architectural Acoustics," *Journal of the Acoustical Society of America*, April 1936.

123 Paul Sabine, *Acoustics and Architecture* (New York, McGraw-Hill Book Company, 1932).

124 Paul Sabine, "The Absorption of Sound by Rigid Walls," *Physical Review*, December 1920.

125 "Membership List," *Journal of the Acoustical Society of America*, April 2, 1931.

126 Norman Klein, "Fabyan Seeks to End Din of City Noises," *New York Times*, April 23, 1921

127 Emily Thompson, *The Soundscape of Modernity*.

128 "Theremin-Voxes Heard in Open Air," *New York Times*, August 28, 1928.

ENDNOTES

129 "Radio City Premiere is a Notable Event," *New York Times*, December 28, 1932.

130 Paul Sabine, "Acoustics of Sound Recording Rooms," *Transactions of the Society of Motion Picture Engineers*, July 11, 1939.

131 Donald Crafton, *The Talkies: American Cinema's Transition to Sound, 1926-1931* (New York: Charles Scribner's Sons, 1997).

132 Quote by Kopec in his book, *The Sabines of Riverbank*.

133 Edward W. Kellogg, "Some New Aspects of Reverberation," *Journal of the Society of Motion Picture Engineers*, January 1930.

134 Emily Thompson, *The Soundscape of Modernity*.

135 Emily Thompson, *The Soundscape of Modernity*.

136 Kopec

137 Paul Sabine, "Architectural Acoustics: Its Past and Its Possibilities," *Journal of the Acoustical Society of America*, July 1939.

138 "Noise," *Saturday Review of Literature*, October 24, 1925.

139 William L. Chenery, "The Noise of Civilization," *New York Times Magazine*, February 1, 1920.

140 Emily Thompson, *The Soundscape of Modernity*.

141 Paul Sabine, "The Efficiency of Some Artificial Aids to Hear," *Laryngoscope*, November 1921.

142 Ibid.

143 James Phinney Baxter, *The Greatest of Literary Problems* (Boston: Houghton Mifflin Co., 1915; James Shapiro, *Contested Will: Who Wrote Shakespeare?* (New York: Simon & Schuster, 2010).

144 Francis Bacon, *The Works, Volume IV,* edited by J. Spedding, R.L. Ellis, and D.D. Heath (1901)

145 *The Letters of Thomas Jefferson*, http://www.loc.gov/exhibits/treasures/trm033.html

146 Francis Bacon, *The Works, Volume IV*.

147 Loren Eisley, *The Man Who Saw Through Time* (NY: Scribners, 1973).

148 David Simpson, DePaul University, *Internet Encyclopedia of Philosophy*, http://www.iep.utm.edu/bacon/

149 Arthur Collins, *The English Baronetage* (Tho. Wotton, 1741)

150 William H. Sherman, "How to Make Anything Signify Anything," *Cabinet Magazine*, Winter 2010/11.

151 Francis Bacon, *De Dignitate & Augmentis Scientiarum*, first translated into English by Gilbert Wats as *Of the Advancement and Proficiencie of Learning* (Oxford: Leonard Lichfield, 1640).

152 A. Wigfall Green, *Sir Francis Bacon* (NY: Twayne Publishers, 1966)

153 English translation by James Spedding in 1857.

154 *The Shakespearean Ciphers Examined*.

155 Burrell Ruth in *American Baconiana* of March 1924.

156 Interview with Phyllis Fletcher, who worked at Riverbank in 1917 and 1918. Kopec, *The Sabines of Riverbank*.

157 Interview with Elizabeth Friedman, June 4, 1974. George C. Marshall Foundation.

158 *Hints to the Decipherer of the Greatest Work of Sir Francis Bacon* (Geneva, Illinois: Riverbank Laboratories, 1916).

159 Dorothy Crain, Ciphers for the Little Folks: *A Method of Teaching the Greatest Work of Sir Francis Bacon* (Geneva, Illinois: Riverbank Laboratories, 1916).

160 Louis Kruh, "A Cryptological Travelogue: Riverbank – 1992," *Cryptologia*, Volume XVII, Number 1, January 1993.

ENDNOTES

161 "Was Shakespeare a Rank Imposter?" *Geneva Republican*, March 11, 1916.

162 "Aha! Sherlock is Outdone!" *Chicago Tribune*, April 22, 1916.

163 F.N. D'Alessio, "George Fabyan celebrated for fostering first think tank," Associated Press, June 16, 2001.

164 "Aha! Sherlock is Outdone!" *Chicago Tribune*, April 22, 1916.

165 Ibid.

166 Interview with Elizebeth Friedman, June 4, 1974. George C. Marshall Foundation.

167 *The Shakespearean Ciphers Examined*.

168 Kopec, *The Sabines of Riverbank*

169 *The Shakespearean Ciphers Examined*

170 "Meeting Review," Audio Engineering Society, Chicago Section, October 31, 1901.

171 Kopec, *The Sabines of Riverbank*.

172 Paul Sabine, *Historical Account of the Riverbank Laboratories*.

173 Jane Miller, "Shakespeare Mystery Key in Fabyan Books," *Herald*, August 6, 1939.

174 Kopec, *The Sabines at Riverbank*.

175 Ibid.

176 Ibid.

177 Lambros D. Callimahos, "The Legendary William F. Friedman," *Cyrptologic Spectrum* (Vol. 4, No. 1) Winter 1974.

178 Ronald Clark, *The Man Who Broke Purple: The Life of William F. Friedman, Who Deciphered the Japanese Code in World War II* (Boston: Little, Brown and Company, 1977).

179 Callimahos

GEORGE FABYAN

180 William F. Friedman, "Edgar Allan Poe, Cryptographer," *American Literature*, volume 8, number 3 (1936).

181 Clark.

182 Fabyan letter to Friedman, June 14, 1915. All referenced letters in this chapter are from the George C. Marshall Library at the Virginia Military Institute.

183 "Secret Weapon," *Time Magazine*, May 14, 1956.

184 David Kahn, The Code-Breakers (NY: Scribner, 1967).

185 William H. Sherman, "How to Make Anything Signify Anything," *Cabinet Magazine*, Winter 2010/11.

186 Clark

187 John Ellis, *The Social History of the Machine Gun*, (Baltimore: Johns Hopkins University Press, 1986), pp 16-17

188 G.J. Meyer, *A World Undone: The Story of the Great War, 1914 to 1918*, (NY: Delacorte, 2006) p. 376

189 John Bourne, "Total War I: The Great War," in *The Oxford History of Modern War*, ed. Charles Townshend, p. 131 (Oxford, Oxford University Press, 2005)

190 Kahn, p 299

191 Winston Churchill, *The World Crisis* (New York: Charles Scribner's Sons, 1923), at I, 503.

192 Kahn, p. 272

193 Kahn, p. 278

194 Kahn, p. 279

195 Churchill III, 112

196 William F. Friedman and Dr. Charles J. Mendelsohn, *The Zimmerman Telegram of January 16, 1917 and its Cryptographic*

ENDNOTES

Background, War Department, Office of the Chief Signal Officer (Washington, D.C.: U.S. Government Printing Office, 1938).

197 Barbara Tuchman, *The Zimmerman Telegram* (New York: Viking Press, 1958) p 184-187.

198 Kahn, p 297

199 Clark.

200 Clark.

201 Clark.

202 Clark.

203 Letter from Fabyan (on Bliss, Fabyan & Co. letterhead) to Military Intelligence, March 15, 1917. Marshall Library.

204 Clark

205 Interview with Elizebeth Friedman, June 4, 1974. George C. Marshall Foundation.

206 *An Introduction to Methods for the Solution of Ciphers*. Publication No. 17. (Geneva, Illinois: Riverbank Laboratories, Department of Ciphers, 1918).

207 Ibid.

208 Ibid

209 *The Index of Coincidence and Its Applications in Cryptography*. (Paris: Imprimerie-Librairie Militaire Universelle, 1922).

210 *Methods for The Solution of Running-Key Ciphers*. Publication No. 16. (Geneva, Illinois: Riverbank Laboratories, Department of Ciphers, 1918).

211 Letter from Fabyan to Col. R.H. Van Deman, November 26, 1917. Marshall Library.

212 Clark.

213 Frank Moorman, "Wireless Intelligence," Lecture delivered to the Military Intelligence Division, General Staff, February 13, 1920.

214 Kahn p. 369

215 Friedman, "Field Codes Used by the German Army during the World War."

216 Ibid

217 Memo from Major Yardley to General Churchill, August 14, 1919.

218 William Friedman, "Memorandum Regarding the Riverbank Publications," Undated.

219 Friedman letter to Fabyan (from France; five-page letter), December 9, 1918.

220 Friedman letter to Fabyan, December 9, 1918.

221 Fabyan letter to Friedman, December 12, 1918

222 Friedman letter to Fabyan, December 9, 1918.

223 Friedman early 1921 letter to Dr. Manly, a former colleague and then Herbert Yardley's second-in-command at the Black Chamber.

224 Fabyan letter to Elizabeth Friedman, January 6, 1919.

225 Fabyan letter to Friedman, September 21, 1918.

226 Clark.

227 Fabyan letter to Lt. Col. Clem Trott, October 20, 1920.

228 Interview with Elizabeth Friedman, June 4, 1974. George C. Marshall Foundation.

229 Fabyan letter to Friedman, November 13, 1918.

230 Letter from Friedman to Fabyan, December 9, 1918.

231 Fabyan letter to AT&T, March 22, 1919.

232 General Churchill letter to Fabyan, August 8, 1919.

233 Clark, p. 76

ENDNOTES

234 Clark, p. 76

235 Major Mauborgne letter to Friedman, November 27, 1920.

236 Friedman to Major Mauborgne, night letter, October 22, 1920.

237 Friedman letter to Major Mauborgne, (confidential letter sent by special delivery) November 19, 1920.

238 Interview with Elizebeth Friedman, June 4, 1974. George C. Marshall Foundation.

239 Clark

240 Friedman letter to Eisenhour, June 8, 1921.

241 Lambros D. Callimahos, "The Legendary William F. Friedman." *Cryptologic Spectrum* (Vol. 4, No. 1) Winter 1974.

242 Clark

243 Clark.

244 *Toronto Mail and Empire*, January 9, 1930

245 Quote by Lambros Callimahos, "The Legendary William F. Friedman." *Cryptologic Spectrum* (Vol. 4, No. 1) Winter 1974.

246 Quote by John Friedman in James R. Chiles, "Breaking codes was this couple's lifetime career," *Smithsonian,* June 1987.

247 *Smithsonian,* June 1987.

248 Clark.

249 Fabyan letter to Friedman, April 2, 1921.

250 Fabyan letter to Friedman, January 12, 1922.

251 Fabyan letter to Friedman, March 2, 1921.

252 Friedman letter to Fabyan, March 10, 1921.

253 Tona Kunz, "Fabyan Estate's designation uncertain," *Kane County Chronicle,* May 22, 1998.

254 Kopec

255 Letter to Wilmer Bartholomew; August 1, 1958.

256 Ronald Clark, *The Man Who Broke Purple: The Life of William F. Friedman, Who Deciphered the Japanese Code in World War II* (Boston: Little, Brown and Company, 1977).

257 Clark

258 William F. and Elizebeth S. Friedman, *The Shakespearean Ciphers Examined* (London: Cambridge University Press, 1958)

259 Ibid.

260 Ibid.

261 Ibid

262 Ibid

263 Ibid.

264 Ibid.

265 Ibid.

266 The Center for Cryptologic History, *The Friedman Legacy* (Fort Meade, Maryland: National Security Agency, 1992).

267 Clark, page 158.

268 Clark, page 166

269 Clark, page 171.

270 Jerrold and Leona Schecter, *Sacred Secrets*, (Washington, D.C.: Brassey's, 2002).

271 Clark

272 Remarks by William Crowell at CIA Headquarters on July 11, 1995.

273 John Early Haynes and Harvey Klehr, *Venona: Decoding Soviet Espionage in America* (New Haven: Yale University Press, 2000) p 12

274 "FBI Office Memorandum; A.H. Belmont to L.V. Boardman," February 1956. http://cryptome.org/fbi-nsa.htm.

ENDNOTES

275 Daniel Patrick Moynihan, *Secrecy: The American Experience,* (New Haven: Yale University Press, 1998).

276 James R. Chiles, *Smithsonian Magazine.*

277 Clark, page 249.

278 Clark

279 Clark, page 258.

280 Friedman letter to William Bundy, Henry Stimson's biographer.

281 Clark, page 260.

282 "Col. Fabyan Dies; Science Patron." *Chicago Herald,* May 19, 1936.

283 "History Behind Fabyan Preserve," *Aurora Beacon-News*, June 12, 1954.

Made in the USA
Charleston, SC
12 October 2013